Peace Out of Reach

Peace Out of Reach

Middle Eastern Travels and the Search for Reconciliation

Stephen Eric Bronner

THE UNIVERSITY PRESS OF KENTUCKY

Publication of this volume was made possible in part by a grant from the National Endowment for the Humanities.

Scholarly publisher for the Commonwealth, serving Bellarmine University, Berea College, Centre College of Kentucky, Eastern Kentucky University, The Filson Historical Society, Georgetown College, Kentucky Historical Society, Kentucky State University, Morehead State University, Murray State University, Northern Kentucky University, Transylvania University, University of Kentucky, University of Louisville, and Western Kentucky University.

Editorial and Sales Offices: The University Press of Kentucky
663 South Limestone Street, Lexington, Kentucky 40508-4008
www.kentuckypress.com

11 10 09 08 07 5 4 3 2 1

Library of Congress Cataloging-in-Publication Data
Bronner, Stephen Eric, 1949-
Peace out of reach : Middle Eastern travels and the search for reconciliation / Stephen Eric Bronner.
p. cm.
Includes bibliographical references and index.
ISBN 978-0-8131-2446-9 (hardcover : alk. paper)
1. Middle East--Politics and government—1979- 2. Conflict management—Middle East. I. Title.
DS63.1.B76 2007
956.05—dc22
2007003155

This book is printed on acid-free recycled paper meeting the requirements of the American National Standard for Permanence in Paper for Printed Library Materials.

Manufactured in the United States of America.

Member of the Association of American University Presses

In Memory of Christian Fenner (1942–2006)

Contents

Acknowledgments ix
1 Cosmopolitan Engagements 1
2 Lessons from Afghanistan 13
3 The Iraqi Debacle: Democracy, Desperation, and the Ethics of War 25
4 Twilight in Tehran 41
5 Syria and Its President: A Meeting with Bashar al-Assad 59
6 Withdrawal Pains: Gaza, Lebanon, and the Future of Palestine 75
7 The Middle East Spills Over: The Sudan and the Crisis in Darfur 93
8 Conspiracy Then and Now: History, Politics, and the Anti-Semitic Imagination 109
9 Incendiary Images: Blasphemous Cartoons, Cosmopolitan Responsibility, and Critical Engagement 123
10 Of Reason and Faith: On the Former Cardinal Josef Ratzinger 135
11 False Antinomies: On Religious Conviction and Human Rights 147
Notes 161
Index 179

Acknowledgments

I would like to express my thanks to the people who helped bring this book to fruition. Lawrence Davidson, Robert Fitch, Kurt Jacobsen, and Michael Thompson spent their valuable time reading drafts of the text and offering excellent comments and criticisms. Linda Lotz was very helpful with copyediting the manuscript, and Stephen Wrinn and Anne Dean Watkins at the University Press of Kentucky were simply wonderful. Finally, once again, I would like to give special thanks to my wife, Anne Burns, for her insight and support.

1

Cosmopolitan Engagements

As I am writing these lines, sitting at my desk, U.S. foreign policy in the Middle East has already unraveled. Afghanistan is witnessing the resurgence of the Taliban, Iraq is disintegrating, Iran is at loggerheads with the West, Syria has retreated further from democracy, Hezbollah and Hamas have captured the imagination of the Arab world, and conflict in the Sudan is producing a nightmare for Darfur. Anti-Semitism is witnessing a rebirth, chauvinism and provincialism are on the rise, and religious intolerance is again contesting the Enlightenment legacy. U.S. foreign policy in those Islamic states gripped by crisis (or the prospect of crisis) now consists of little more than calls for economic sanctions or threats of military action. Most of the world looks with dismay at the results of American interventions in Afghanistan and Iraq, the threats directed against Iran and Syria, the United States' uncritical support for Israeli policy in Palestine and Lebanon, its disregard for human rights, and what has become its open contempt for the will of the international community. As a result of all this, the standing of liberals and moderates in the Middle East has declined, fragile states have become more fragile, terror has been embraced as a legitimate tactic, and the Unites States has been left without genuine diplomatic influence on any regional actor other than Israel. The Bush administration has opened a Pandora's box through its self-righteous posturing and its belief that democracy can be imposed by a policy of "shock and awe." The United States has contributed nothing toward resolving the regional conflagration sparked by the discrete political crises and ideological conflicts discussed in this book.

Introducing the need for a different approach is the purpose behind *Peace Out of Reach.* As in so many other fields of inquiry, however, the general interpretation of foreign policy has made way for empirical and relatively technical works dedicated to examining the crisis of the moment. This trend has had a debilitating impact on public discussion and the development of a strategic intelligence among the citizenry at large. Indeed, even when a more general perspective is provided, it usually comes in the form of a huge tome that is undoubtedly consulted episodically rather than read through with care. Either brevity or clarity is sacrificed. Here, by way of contrast, I hope to provide a broad perspective and a set of interconnected studies pertaining to the symbolic and practical politics generated in the Middle East that are readable, empirically grounded, speculatively realistic, and politically to the point.

Peace Out of Reach is equally informed by my academic research and activism. Originally, my scholarly concerns revolved around the European labor movement, fascism, anti-Semitism, and Western political theory beginning with the Enlightenment. I learned much, and my work on these themes shaped my political worldview. My interest in the Middle East grew following the terrorist attack of 9/11, the assault on Afghanistan, and my anger with the misguided policies of the Bush administration. That interest was only intensified by my visits to Iraq—prior to its invasion by the United States—as well as to Iran, Syria, Israel, the Occupied Territories, and the Sudan. My experiences influenced the chapters devoted to each country, if only because my travels had a political component. I participated in what has been termed "citizen diplomacy," in which delegations of American citizens meet unofficially with governmental officials, representatives of nongovernmental organizations, and intellectuals from nations fearful of belligerency by the Bush administration. This activity in conjunction with Faculty for Israeli-Palestinian Peace and groups associated with Conscience International during my visits to Iraq, Iran, and Syria resulted in the writings included here, as well as statements and petitions that may not have shaken the world but were read and signed by tens of thousands of Americans.

Neoconservatives and even some mainstream liberals criticized my colleagues and myself for aiding the enemy and meeting with politicians who had blood on their hands. Little did it matter that these trips were undertaken with no external financial backing or that we prided ourselves on our independence from the U.S. government as well as from the states and officials we visited. Some partisans of the Right insisted that the very act of visiting rogue states or speaking with dictators necessarily turned us into their apologists. It is exactly this kind of "us versus them" mentality that lies at the root of every provincial and authoritarian understanding of politics. A right-wing student of mine said that the problem with my analysis of Israeli politics was that it didn't evidence any particular "love" for that country. But politics is neither a soccer game nor the love boat. It requires objectivity, holding the emotional claims of both sides at a distance, and a willingness to learn about nations and cultures foreign to our own. My friends and I believed that our attempt to foster dialogue with people different from us and with officials who did not always share our basic beliefs was honorable, ethical, and extremely instructive.

Perhaps we were "manipulated." That is, perhaps the media in Iraq, Iran, and Syria portrayed us as critical of U.S. foreign policy—but we *were* critical of U.S. policy. Is it legitimate for American citizens to make these criticisms only on American soil? That we offered our opinions on a foreign stage did not imply that, somehow surreptitiously, we were providing an apology for dictators and aiding Islamic fascism. None of us played the role of what Lenin termed the "useful idiot," and we never romanticized the "other" in the manner of days gone by. Our statements, in fact, expressed dismay over the constriction of civil liberties and sharp criticisms of the authoritarian states we visited. Our explicit aims were to help correct the misinformation generated by the American media and prevent the United States from arbitrarily exercising its military power without regard for international law, the national interest, or the everyday people who suffer the consequences.

There is no need for pretense: spending a week or two in this or that nation does not transform a guest into an expert. But these trips were invaluable for me in terms of learning how American intentions are perceived, understanding the anger produced by double standards, and fostering what I have called elsewhere a "cosmopolitan sensibility." My visits allowed me to encounter directly some of those who would bear the costs of American foreign policy, and I gained a new understanding of what the military blithely refers to as "collateral damage."

There is something else that needs to be said: Americans seem incapable of understanding the sinking estimation—and it is, according to numerous mainstream polls, still sinking—of their country by so much of the world. These visits clarified for me that, in this vein, Americans must learn more about the "other" if they are to learn anything about themselves. But it works both ways. The states we visited remain very much sealed off from the West and suffer from that peculiar provincialism born of authoritarian rule. Our visits gave our hosts a chance to encounter the "other" as well—hopefully to good effect.

Peace Out of Reach evidences what has always been a cosmopolitan element in my thinking, whose roots surely derive from my background as a child of German-Jewish exiles but also from my appreciation of the European Enlightenment and of those outside of Europe who—like Bolivar, Tagore, and Mandela—sought to foster its radical legacy. As things now stand, it seems as if progressives must navigate between what has often been called the "clash of civilizations." This clash is seen as cultural in character, insofar as it pits a secular and liberal Occident against a rabidly xenophobic and fundamentalist Orient. In my travels it became clear that the real clash is the one that pits secular and liberal elements against nationalist and fundamentalist elements in both the West and the East.

Imperialism has undercut the insularity of these two regions, and the interaction between them will grow due to increased opportunities for travel, information sharing, and communication. Modernity will undoubtedly penetrate traditional societies and create new opportunities for democratic change. But these must ultimately develop organically rather than through the intrusion of nations with new imperialist ambitions and officials virtually bereft of knowledge about the societies they wish to transform. Citizen diplomacy can prove useful in this regard. Building bridges and creating linkages between those with similar values on both sides of the divide is, in my view, the task of the cosmopolitan in a post-9/11 world.

Peace Out of Reach is predicated on the practical need to judge foreign policy according to criteria that are cosmopolitan and democratic. The introduction of such concerns is perhaps a product of the Vietnam War. Prior to the 1960s, there had been relatively little domestic protest against the numerous interventions undertaken by the United States since it entered the world stage as a great power in 1898. The framers of foreign policy basically engaged in secret diplomacy outside the public purview. That changed irrevocably not only because of the

American defeat in Vietnam, which left a lasting imprint on my generation, but also because of the advent of the Internet and the possibility of a genuinely global exchange of information. The "war on terror" has also shown that large-scale undertakings in foreign policy demand more than a national consensus. They require international support as well. Commitment to building a cosmopolitan sensibility is therefore no longer a luxury; it is a necessity in achieving that kind of support.

First introduced in my book *Ideas in Action*, the cosmopolitan sensibility should not be understood as a purely formal philosophical category or a purely legal commitment to universal human rights. Immanuel Kant originally defined cosmopolitanism as the ability to feel at home everywhere. The sensibility projected by this idea is thus informed by empathy for those "others" who bear the costs of political action. The cosmopolitan sensibility provides a social content to human rights, even as it highlights the moment of solidarity in resisting the exercise of arbitrary power and the dead weight of provincial traditions. It also presumes the goodwill necessary to step outside oneself, criticize the cruder forms of national interest, and engage the "other" in a meaningful dialogue. In terms of foreign policy, therefore, the cosmopolitan sensibility requires that any genuinely democratic undertaking be transparent and accountable with respect to the material interests and ethical intentions informing it and that moral and practical limits be placed on what is permissible. In the United States, since the Vietnam War, foreign policy has been subjected to a new public morality that insists on transparency and accountability and that poses a direct challenge to the arbitrary and unilateral exercise of power in foreign affairs.

Sadly, the Bush administration never really accepted any of this. Committed to a self-serving globalism rather than cosmopolitanism, its officials lied to the American public and to the international community as the invasion of Iraq became imminent. Neither the material interests nor the ethical intentions of the United States in pursuing its war on terror were ever made transparent. Misinformation about the aims of the war on terror and the threat to national security was combined with the imperialist quest for oil and geopolitical advantage, support for Israel, and billions of dollars in contracts to favored corporations. A peculiar arrogance informed the twin beliefs that only the United States—and perhaps a few of its close allies—has the right to engage in a preemptive strike and that doing so will evoke limitless gratitude from liberated peoples who wish only "to be like us."

In my view, ideas like these, as much as any form of military incompetence, produced a lack of concern about the broader implications of regime change or the development of an exit strategy in Iraq. Such provincial arrogance on the part of neoconservatives and certain liberals also made it difficult for them to appreciate how other nations understand the widespread use of torture at prisons such as Abu Ghraib and Guantanamo Bay and the daily attacks by Americans on Iraqi civilians. It also informed their spin on the massacres in towns such as Haditha, the ruthless carnage inflicted on Falluja, the rubble that is now Ramadi, and the environmental disaster unleashed through depleted uranium, multiple oil spills, and the pollution of the Tigris. There is little sense of how all this can be identified with the original attempt to foster democracy or fulfill the United States' mission for the region. In the eyes of the world, the foreign policy of the Bush administration increasingly resembles that of a corporate thug—half obsessed with power and half paranoid at the thought of that power being challenged. This has led to erosion of the international support for the United States following the 9/11 attacks.

Style counts in foreign affairs. The international community views the Bush administration as unconcerned with the opinions of other states, convinced of its moral superiority, and intent on having its own way no matter what the costs to others. Its style is to make plans in secret, treat critics as enemies, and—even with half a trillion dollars spent on defense every year—continually insist that U.S. national security is threatened. Paranoia mixes with belligerency. Diplomacy appears to be little more than a kind of unsatisfying foreplay that, form dictates, must occur prior to the real thing: the preemptive strike. Of course, it's not as if the Democratic Party has developed much of an alternative in foreign affairs. Most of its major representatives are equally culpable for the resentment of the world community, given their support of an ill-defined war on terror and the invasion of Iraq. Nevertheless, it remains important to distinguish between neoconservative ideologues bent on a mission of world salvation and cowed liberal politicians standing just a bit to the left of their xenophobic rivals while content to follow the leader.

True believers come in many varieties—some believe in their religion, some in their nation, some in their ethnic community—but they share much in common. What marks them all is a lack of concern for the "other," a conviction that their belief is uniquely privileged, a dogmatic sensitivity to criticism, and a willingness to sacrifice their fellow citizens in the name of their state, their house of worship, or their particular organization. In their view, the "people" become identified with the institution and its ambitions. What marks the cosmopolitan sensibility, however, is the refusal to accept at face value that kind of identification or the legitimacy of those "sacrifices" that true believers always demand. Recognition of constraints, costs, and the balance of power thus becomes more important than romantic slogans about "struggle" and the liberating missions of great powers that usually harbor imperialist ambitions. The cosmopolitan sensibility rests on emphasizing reciprocity, rejecting the use of a double standard, and placing moral limits on action. The principal concern of the cosmopolitan is not the interests of states, religious institutions, or various organizations but the interests of those who will suffer as a result of the decisions made by true believers in their name.

Unclear about the enemy, unconcerned with international law, inclined to inflate the implications of every conflict, and profoundly ignorant of the radically different cultural and historical traditions in the nations making up the world community, the true believers in the Bush administration have crudely pursued their war on terror. They have little sense of the need for modest aims and a realistic assessment of constraints. These elements are especially important when dealing with nations in the Middle East that have been subject to Western imperialism and lack a democratic tradition, an indigenous bourgeoisie, and a viable civil society. Perhaps Vice President Dick Cheney and his neoconservative cabal really believed that simply toppling the regime of Saddam Hussein would cause democracy to flourish. More likely, their concern was to secure a geopolitical advantage for the United States in the Middle East, establish military bases, and control oil, while eliminating yet another enemy of Israel. What counts, in any event, is the way the American national interest was betrayed and the price that is still being paid by the citizens of the Middle East.

Peace Out of Reach critically examines the assumptions behind an ethically suspect and politically misguided foreign policy, the costs of what have been clumsily portrayed as altruistic attempts to export democracy, and emerging ideological trends fueled by cultural insensitivity, anti-Semitism, and fear of the Enlightenment legacy. It is concerned with curbing unbridled ambitions and inhibiting those passions associated with intolerance and violence. That is possible only by recognizing the limits of power and resisting the attempts—as one Bush official so delicately put it—to "make reality" as the reigning superpower and its allies see fit.

Peace Out of Reach calls on policy makers to demonstrate a plausible connection between the ends they seek and the means they use to realize them. The idea that the end justifies the means has always rested on casuistry. It only begs the question of what justifies the end, and to this question, there can be only one answer: the means used to achieve it. Neoconservatives like to claim that the democratic Iraq of the future will justify the sacrifices made in the present. Of course, with an eye trained on the American public, they fail to mention that it is the Iraqis who must live with the devastation. Even if a democratic order ultimately emerged in Iraq, the dozens of cities destroyed, the environmental devastation, the hundreds of thousands driven from their homes, and the many tens of thousands of Iraqi deaths required to achieve it—one hundred per day, and fourteen thousand in the first six months of 2006—have already rendered the cost too high. It is not the case that the foreign policy of the Bush administration is an expression of the national interest, that it has made areas of geopolitical importance more secure, and that it has promoted not merely democracy but also a democratic way of life.

Democracy involves more than elections. It also depends on the practice of civil liberties, some degree of social justice, a diverse civil society, and a general spirit of reciprocity and tolerance. Virtually nowhere in the Middle East have these preconditions for democratic change been strengthened. Its ruling elites are anachronisms, and the United States is paying a high price in Arab public opinion—what is known as the Arab "street"—for supporting them. Liberal hawks and conservative dogmatists have converged in their refusal to consider the structural constraints existing in those nations they wish to transform. No state with artificially drawn borders and without an indigenous bourgeoisie, a democratic labor movement, and a liberal political tradition has ever been turned into a democracy overnight. Building democracy in such states requires an organic development *from within.* That development is capable of being nurtured but incapable of being forced. As *Peace Out of Reach* suggests, to ignore this reality is to indulge in the illusion of power.

2

Lessons from Afghanistan

September 11, 2001, marked the beginning of a new millennium.[1] It was a traumatic event for all who lived through it, even those who did not lose family or friends but merely watched the tragedy on television. Not since the attack on Pearl Harbor in 1941 had the United States been struck by an enemy on its own soil. This particular enemy was not even a nation-state but rather an international terrorist movement, al Qaeda, inspired by a rigidly anachronistic version of Islam and led by Osama bin Laden. Americans' initial shock and sadness quickly turned to anger. Little time was spent reflecting on the supposed reasons for the attack on the World Trade Center and the Pentagon—namely, U.S. support for corrupt Arab regimes such as those of Saudi Arabia and Egypt, as well as support for Israeli policy with regard to the Palestinians. Talk of revenge was rampant, and there was a sense, legitimate or not, of innocence violated. Hatred of Islamic fundamentalism intensified, and the belief in an inevitable conflict between Occident and Orient, or what neoconservatives such as Bernard Lewis and Samuel Huntington termed a "clash of civilizations," gripped the popular imagination. There was never any doubt that the United States should seek retribution for the victims of 9/11. This was the context in which the United States decided to bomb Afghanistan and overthrow its Islamic fundamentalist leadership—the Taliban—which was openly protecting bin Laden and al Qaeda.

International law does not deny a nation the right to defend itself when attacked.[2] President George Bush insisted that Afghanistan hand over every terrorist, close every training facility, and give the United States the authority to carry out inspections.[3] These were difficult demands for the Taliban to accept. But rejecting them meant ignoring both the imperative for action dictated by a national consensus in the United States and support from an international coalition that was appalled by the savage attacks of 9/11. The Taliban clearly misread the situation, and their diplomatic attempts at negotiation were, according to one observer, like "grasping smoke." Their efforts were seen as a form of stalling. The Bush administration wished to act quickly, and its desire to avenge a criminal act against innocent civilians and bring the culprits to justice—if not begin a "war on terror" against an ill-defined enemy—initially seemed reasonable.

Attacking Afghanistan did not eliminate al Qaeda, whose transnational organization has appropriately been called a "network of networks." But the bombing of Afghanistan succeeded in destroying a number of training bases and a barbaric regime that had served as an important sanctuary for al Qaeda.[4] Militants such as Osama bin Laden and the leader of the Taliban, Mullah Omar, were forced to go underground, flee to remote areas, or retreat into Pakistan. Soon, however, the United States seemed to lose interest in finding these new celebrities. More importantly, four thousand Afghan civilians were killed, tens of thousands were wounded, and half a million were left homeless.[5] These numbers dwarf the numbers of Americans killed and wounded by the assault of 9/11. It forces any decent person to at least consider what Albert Camus called the "principle of reasonable culpability" when engaging in military action, as well as the practical and moral costs of ignoring it.

Whether this imbalance in sacrifice and lack of proportionality could have been avoided, or whether different military procedures should have been undertaken, remains an open question. Indisputable, however, is the fact that the Taliban regime was willing to sacrifice its citizens rather than hand over the criminals responsible for 9/11. Parceling out guilt always seems both grotesque and futile. But it is important to understand that the Taliban was complicit in what transpired in the nation it ruled. The burden of culpability does not fall only on the United States. Nevertheless, given the lack of proportionality in terms of the sacrifices made by the citizens of Afghanistan and those of the United States, it is necessary to highlight the importance that should have been attached to the reconstruction of Afghanistan.[6]

Even after Kabul fell, the United States still possessed the moral high ground. Its demand for justice, for the prosecution of Osama bin Laden and his band of criminals, was accompanied by promises of if not state building then at least the reconstruction of Afghanistan. But these promises were never kept. Social and economic reconstruction took a backseat to searching for bin Laden and creating a huge military base in the center of the world's largest oil-producing region that was intended, quite obviously, to allow the United States to intervene there at will. In the north of Afghanistan, admittedly, new educational and cultural freedoms took root as many refugees returned to their homes. The economy grew by 14 percent in 2005,[7] but this figure is deceiving. In the east and the south, public infrastructure is still a shambles, and 80 percent of the population is illiterate. Even worse, by 2006, 10 percent of the Afghan population was living off food aid, and government revenue amounted to only 5.4 percent of the nondrug gross domestic product. In 2005 the government raised only $300 million in revenue, whereas the total budget was roughly $5 billion.[8] The difference had to be supplied by external sources, and the Bush administration provided $2 billion in 2006. Economic reconstruction also lagged due to the lack of electrical power, an inadequate infrastructure, and the prevailing political instability that the U.S. occupation has failed to relieve. The reason is fairly obvious: Afghanistan became a "sideshow" as the focus of U.S. policy shifted to Iraq.[9]

This is clearly revealed in a discussion that took place on February 19, 2002, between Senator Bob Graham of Florida and General Tommy Franks.[10] At the time, the former was the chair of the Senate Select Intelligence Committee, and the latter was the head of U.S. Central Command. Franks apparently told Graham, "we are not engaged in a war in Afghanistan . . . [and] military and intelligence personnel are being redeployed to prepare for an action in Iraq." Graham apparently replied that he was "stunned" to learn that "the decision to go to war with Iraq had not only been made but was being implemented to the substantial disadvantage of the war in Afghanistan." What this suggests, of course, is that the Iraq war appreciably weakened the fight against the real enemy: al Qaeda and the criminal organizations that launched the attacks of 9/11.

There is something genuinely shocking about this conversation.[11] It evidences the basic lack of leadership concerning the war, its goals, and the particular enemy to be defeated in both Afghanistan and Iraq. Those two nations, it should be noted, now rank tenth and fourth, respectively, in the "failed states index" composed by Foreign Policy and the Fund for Peace. In Afghanistan, no less than in Iraq, regime change was not difficult for the United States to achieve. But the United States' ability to prevent the resurgence of the enemy is another matter entirely. Only a handful of cities in Afghanistan have actually been secured, and that situation, whether due to a lack of adequate forces or poor strategic planning, has been replicated time and again in Iraq. A city is conquered militarily by U.S. forces, which are then immediately deployed elsewhere, thereby allowing the enemy to regroup. Unwilling to rethink the strategy that has failed so miserably in the past, the United States has responded to a worsening conflict by placing another twelve thousand troops under NATO's command.[12] Thus, fourteen thousand of the thirty-two thousand NATO troops in Afghanistan have been supplied by the United States in what is the largest deployment of American troops under foreign command since the Second World War. Whether this will change anything is doubtful. Lieutenant General David Richards, the senior British military official in charge of NATO forces, has already stated publicly that Afghanistan is "close to anarchy."[13]

From the beginning, some had an uncomfortable feeling that the Bush administration might not view 9/11 principally as a criminal act; that it might take this single legitimate reason for retaliation and use it as the basis for other imperialist exploits and as an excuse for a universal war on terror without end and without a definite enemy.[14] That intuition proved correct. Plans for the invasion of Iraq were already on President Bush's desk on September 12, 2001, and from the start, Afghanistan was part of a broader American strategy that involved more than the capture of Osama bin Laden and the uprooting of al Qaeda. Afghan citizens would pay a high price for their liberation from the Taliban. Aside from the thousands killed and the tens of thousands injured in the initial bombing campaign, the economy has collapsed to the point where various estimates suggest that 40 percent of the population is living below the subsistence level.

This dire situation has other causes besides the regime change brought about by the United States. More than a million Afghanis had already died in the war with the Soviet

Union and the civil war that ensued after the withdrawal of Soviet troops and the collapse of its puppet regime in 1992. Afghanistan was fractured into discrete regions run by tribal chieftains or warlords in a state of conflict. Under these circumstances, close to one-third of the population fled, with about two million Afghanis settling in Iran and another three million in Pakistan.[15] With strong ties to the Pashtun community in the south of Afghanistan, the Taliban had little trouble conquering the southern provinces, where they have surfaced once again as a dominant political force and have shown few qualms about slaughtering their opponents or ruling with the iron hand of religious certainty. It was only with the victory of the Taliban, which probably came closest to uniting the country, that Osama bin Laden moved his operation to Afghanistan.[16] Recourse to a religious ideology was the logical alternative for a devastated nation bereft of economic hope, where liberal nationalism was an abstraction and socialism was identified with the Russian invader. This explains not only the original appeal of the Taliban, whose leaders emerged from the religious schools that flowered in Pakistan, but also the rise of fundamentalism throughout a region whose peoples see themselves as victims of economic globalization.

Elections took place in Afghanistan on September 18, 2005. There was less bloodshed than anticipated, and it should be noted that an extraordinary number of women became members of parliament. Fifty-three percent of the citizenry voted; this was about 20 percent less than in the presidential elections of 2004 but still a very high turnout, considering that only parliamentary seats were at stake. This does not change the fact that the country remains dominated by different ethnic groups to the point where one analyst suggested that "there are no Afghans in Afghanistan. . . . Nationalism is a meaningless notion; loyalty is to tribe or clan—not to a central authority."[17]

Under these circumstances, it should not be surprising that nearly 80 percent of the new parliamentary representatives in the provinces and 60 percent in the capital are linked to competing militias and stand accused of various war crimes.[18]

As occurs so often, what was structurally important for the burgeoning democracy of Afghanistan went virtually unreported. Procedures were not established for collecting taxes, and no strategy was articulated for either disarming the militias or dealing with the Taliban.[19] The new parliament was organized not around parties but around individuals. This might appear to have strengthened the hand of President Hamid Karzai, but only in relation to the parliament, and only in the area around the capital. Because warlords and drug lords still effectively run much of the country,[20] Karzai retains his power only insofar as he can rally them to his project and employ their militias for his own purposes. Afghanistan has thus turned into a patchwork of warlord-controlled fiefdoms, and insofar as Karzai relies on these petty tyrants, his own power has become circumscribed and his legitimacy is suspect.[21] The result for Afghanistan has been a variant of what Trotsky called "dual power." Karzai substantively dominates the formal rule of parliament, but the formal rule of Karzai is contradicted by the substantive power exercised by the conflicting forces of a traditional civil society. Here is the parallel with Iraq. American policy makers now fear that the Iraqi insurgency—with its organized bombings, kidnappings, and murders (especially of the educated representatives of civil society) by a combination of genuine nationalists, crime bosses, and ethnic and religious fanatics—will provide a model for what happens in Afghanistan.

Five years after the attack on the World Trade Center and the Pentagon, most Americans can still barely identify the nation that protected those considered culpable for that atrocity.[22] In the popular imagination, al Qaeda is still coupled with the Iraq of Saddam Hussein, and only secondarily with Afghanistan and its former Taliban regime. When the Senate observed a minute of silence to remember the 2,500 fallen American soldiers in Iraq (before voting against a "cut and run" strategy), it completely forgot about the 250 American soldiers who lost their lives in Afghanistan. Perhaps that only makes sense, given that media coverage of Afghanistan has also declined precipitously. ABC, CBS, and NBC together devoted 306 minutes to covering that tiny but geopolitically important nation in November 2001; that was down to 28 minutes by February 2003 and less than 1 minute a month later, even though Afghanistan had already been the subject of military invasion.[23] That began to change with the resurgence of the Taliban, but neglect of Afghanistan was renewed with the Israel-Lebanon war of 2006. Coverage will undoubtedly increase once again with the growing number of casualties and the instability of the regime led by President Karzai. The question is whether it will highlight the important lessons provided by Afghanistan with respect to the misguided character of U.S. foreign policy and the precipitous decline of American prestige in the world community.

Afghanistan illustrates the need for a kind of critical radar with respect to how the emotions of a citizenry, understandably heightened by a terrible tragedy, can be manipulated. Although the desire for retribution for the victims of 9/11 retained legitimacy, it also overshadowed other interests that should have been made transparent. For instance, there has been a lack of media exposure and critical inquiry about the military bases constructed in Afghanistan and the many more built in central Asia, as the United States strives to control the resources in the region and encircle the Persian Gulf.[24] Coming on the heels of 9/11, it was quite apparent that the difficulties of the undertaking in Afghanistan had been underestimated. The experience in Afghanistan shows the implausibility of assuming that regime change—even when the regime is as noxious as the Taliban—will suddenly usher in a viable democracy.

In Afghanistan—as in Iraq—President George Bush and his supporters showed little prudence when they prematurely declared victory. Both countries lacked mass-based organizations committed to democratic government, and there was little anticipation that American intervention would generate guerrilla movements among the civilian population or intensify the ethnic and religious conflicts simmering within these traditional societies. Whatever the "grand game," American policy makers could not articulate what it meant to either complete a military mission or transfer power to the new regime and make good on an exit strategy. The absence of any foundation for a stable, secular, democratic regime remains notable in both nations, and it is increasingly difficult to accept claims that either intervention constitutes a success story.

Afghanistan also provides a classic example of what Chalmers Johnson called "blowback."[25] Osama bin Laden was originally what he termed a "protégé" of the United States, and it was the Reagan administration's decision to support the mujahideen, or essentially any group resisting the Soviet Union's occupation of Afghanistan, that first produced al Qaeda and the Taliban.[26] As suggested by the disaster that followed, the enemy of my enemy is not necessarily my friend. Afghanistan shows the importance of thinking beyond the moment and beyond a shortsighted and morally shallow "realism" and the importance of acknowledging the danger of being defined by what one opposes.

In Afghanistan—as in Iraq—the enemy will not simply disappear. The Taliban is rooted in parts of the Afghan community, and simply sending more troops is not the answer. Either U.S. foreign policy will negotiate with the enemy, with an eye toward integrating the Taliban into a new political order, or the United States will find itself embroiled in yet another quagmire. The time to undertake this new direction in U.S. foreign policy toward Afghanistan is not later but now.

Even as the Bush administration shifted the material costs for its decision to end the barbaric rule of the Taliban and Saddam Hussein to the peoples of Afghanistan and Iraq, it continued to present the United States as bearing the heaviest burden. Or, to put it another way, the Bush administration has refused to take responsibility for the collapse of democratic possibilities following the original interventions, even though it has presented the United States as the agent of democratic liberation. A refusal to acknowledge both the imbalance of sacrifices and the consequences of its own decisions has dramatically undermined the moral standing of the United States.

Part and parcel of all this, in my view, was American officials' cynical unwillingness to consider placing limits on the exercise of power, or what Hannah Arendt termed "the boundlessness of action." Torture is the most extreme expression of the limitless exercise of power and action without boundaries. The degree to which it is prevalent is the degree to which a police state exists. Concepts such as proportionality and limits are embedded in any liberal understanding of the rule of law.[27] Denial of the notions of proportionality and limits by radical fundamentalists or anti-Western nationalists who are willing to murder or torture their enemies, whether military or civilian, does not excuse the denial of those notions by right-wing fanatics in the United States who constantly trumpet their commitment to humane values.

Before the scandal broke about the prison at Abu Ghraib, torture and abuse of prisoners in Afghanistan had already become more than merely an aberration in the "normal" activities of the military.[28] Prisoners captured by the U.S. military were regularly sent to facilities in allied nations with abysmal human rights records in what has become known as "rendition." Reports of torture by American troops are numerous, but perhaps one deserves particular mention. Eight different accounts, consistent in their most important aspects, were given by men imprisoned at Guantanamo Bay, who told of being held at a secret prison in Afghanistan from 2002 until 2004. Human Rights Watch reported that these men were kept hungry, chained to the walls, and in total darkness, with loud music blaring to cause sleep deprivation. Water torture and various other forms of abuse were also apparently employed on a regular basis. Just as important, this prison is one of several, including Camp Eggers in Kabul, the Ariana Hotel, and the infamous military detention center at Bagram, where five hundred "terror suspects" were held under the most brutal conditions.[29] Human Rights Watch insists that the United States has continually and grossly breached the War Crimes Act and antitorture statutes, the laws of Afghanistan, and the International Covenant on Civil and Political Rights.[30]

Many excuses are made for what has become a pattern of torture in the Middle East. They range from the misguided directives emanating from the secretary of defense to soldiers' lengthy deployment in a pressurized battle zone to American troops' learned racist contempt for what have increasingly become enemies of color. But the most frequent excuses either parrot the tautology that we are at war and that torture is to be expected or insist that torture is necessary to extract crucial information that will "save American lives." But if the abused prisoners were Americans, or if another state insisted that it alone had the right to globally pursue those accused of terrorism, the entire United States would be in an uproar. Here we find the double standard employed by the greatest military power, and one that so incenses the world community: what is allowed to "us" must obviously be denied to "them."

If an act of torture really were required to save American lives, then the ethical torturer—a clear oxymoron—would undoubtedly illustrate what was gained by illegal and immoral methods and then accept whatever punishment a court deemed suitable for breaking the law. But real-life torturers hardly ever demonstrate such moral rectitude. That is because they are not moral men and women concerned with larger issues but men and women whose sadistic instincts have been allowed to flourish within a culture of war. Ultimately, the dangerous ease with which that culture can be embraced is the most important lesson taught by the assault on Afghanistan.

3

The Iraqi Debacle

Democracy, Desperation, and the Ethics of War

As a member of U.S. Academics against War, I visited Baghdad and some other Iraqi cities before the bombing began in 2003.[1] It was clear to our group that the justifications offered in support of the attack were at odds with reality. Iraq was a broken-down country still suffering from the effects of the 1991 Gulf War,[2] and it posed no threat to the United States or its national interests. I still remember the brightly lit shops of Baghdad, bustling with activity once the sun went down. There were goods in the stores, schools were functioning, and the streets were safe. Women had entered the social mainstream, the religious attended their mosques, and all raised their families. Life under Saddam Hussein was anything but pleasant, but despite the fear of the police and loathing of the government, people went about their business.

None of this, of course, is the case any longer. Iraq has become a wasteland torn apart by civil war and an insurgency directed against American troops. Even neoconservatives now regret the mistakes—always technical in nature—that were made. But they insist that it is time to forget the past, "support our troops," recognize the chaos that withdrawal will produce, and get behind the Iraqi government installed by the United States. It is virtually the same with that array of right-wing media pundits and their liberal fellow travelers who celebrated victory, chastised critics, called for apologies from the Left, and completely misconceived what was actually taking place.[3]

With the congressional elections of 2006, which resulted in a Democratic takeover of both the House and the Senate, the American people finally expressed their disapproval of the Iraq strategy pursued by the Bush administration. Secretary of Defense Donald Rumsfeld was forced to resign, and UN Ambassador John Bolton relinquished his position. The true dimensions of their terrible policy, however, still remain to be explored. Iraq can serve as a cautionary warning only if such an exploration takes place. The costs to the American psyche will be high. It will require dealing frankly with what will undoubtedly become a memory as painful as the one produced by Vietnam.

On May 1, 2003, President Bush landed on an aircraft carrier and proclaimed victory in Iraq with the words "Mission Accomplished!" The threat to the United States had seemingly passed, the weapons of mass destruction had not been launched, and an ally of al Qaeda had been destroyed. The Baath Party, once headed by Saddam Hussein, had collapsed. Statues of the dictator had tumbled, and Iraqis awaited a democratic regime that was just around the corner. American neoconservatives congratulated themselves on their steely realism, and polls showed that support for the military action had gone through the roof.

Four months after the invasion of Iraq, President Bush explained the reasons for his success. He told a Palestinian delegation headed by then foreign minister Nabil Shaath that God had instructed him to fight the terrorists in Iraq.[4] Apparently, however, God was not the only one whispering in his ear. It seems that the Bush administration relied on information provided by a prisoner—Ibn al-Shaykh al-Libi—who, in keeping with the policy of "rendition," had been handed over to Egypt. And this prisoner, hoping to escape torture, had claimed that ties existed between Iraq and al Qaeda.[5] In any event, there was nothing left for American troops to do but mop up. The situation in Iraq was well in hand.

As for the residual resistance in Iraq, the president would soon invite them to "bring it on!" They brought it on, all right, with or without God on their side, and everyone—including Bush and Blair—now seems to agree that the cry "Mission Accomplished!" was a bit premature.[6] As 2007 begins, American deaths have climbed to over three thousand, and between five and ten times that number have been wounded. But the real victims are the Iraqis. Over the last three years, 100,000 Iraqi men have been detained; most of them were innocent of any wrongdoing, and as of June 2006, "only" 15,000 were still in custody.[7] Middle-class Iraqis have fled to Jordan and other neighboring states by the thousands, and a genuine "brain drain" of Iraqi intellectuals and scientists is currently under way. The population of Falluja fell from 300,000 to 100,000 in the eight weeks of aerial bombardment that preceded the military attack of 2005: 36,000 of the city's 50,000 homes, 8,400 shops, 60 nurseries, and 65 mosques were destroyed.[8] Between 4,000 and 5,000 civilians died, and there is evidence—unreported by the Western press—that white phosphorus was dropped on the city.[9] Other cities such as Mosul and Baghdad were decimated, along with hundreds of mosques, including the famous gold-domed Askariya shrine in Samarra; again, there is "hard evidence" that white phosphorus was deployed against combatants.[10] According to a recent study by the Bloomberg School of Public Health at Johns Hopkins University, between 600,000 and 800,000 citizens in a country of 27 million have been killed since the American invasion of 2003.[11]

Even a minimum of stability is a hope rather than a reality. In terms of the preconditions for a livable future, an independent audit showed that of the $38 billion spent on reconstruction—less than 10 percent of the cost of the war—much has been wasted due to "financial irregularities," bureaucratic infighting, lack of expertise, language ineptitude, lax security, and poor planning.[12] Transparency International, a German nongovernmental organization, listed the Iraqi state as just barely less corrupt than Haiti,[13] and Iraq has been described as the most dangerous society on earth. The social fabric is unraveling amid economic collapse and violence in the streets, and there is simply no evidence that either the new constitution or those who rule in its name have gained the loyalty of the masses. Still intent on "de-Baathification," the present government needs precisely those people whose loyalty it does not command. Meanwhile, elements of an indigenous insurgency are permeating the official armed forces. Shiite death squads have been unleashed against Sunni citizens, and the Sunnis respond in kind. Ethnic and tribal divisions are simmering, and little remains of the vaunted new civil society. The political establishment is deeply divided, there is little identification with the nebulous democratic "national interest," and the former commander of U.S. troops, General John Abizaid, stated publicly that Iraq is sliding into civil war.[14]

Even should a new democratic order rise from the ashes like a phoenix, only the most gruesome exponent of teleology, unconcerned with the real-world suffering of Iraqis across the political spectrum, would say that it was worth it. One new military offensive after another has proved fruitless in quelling the insurgency. Things have only gotten worse with the discovery of death squads inside the Iraqi military, the widespread torturing of Sunnis in Shiite-controlled prisons, ongoing sabotage against oil pipelines and the Iraqi infrastructure, and massacres such as the one at Haditha, where more than two dozen civilians were murdered. Civil war is *already* a reality. Deputy Secretary of Defense Paul Wolfowitz, appearing before a subcommittee of the House of Representatives on February 28, 2003, complained that $12 billion had been spent containing Saddam Hussein since the end of Gulf War I in 1991. Since 2003, based on very conservative estimates, $330 billion has been wasted, the Iraq war is now costing the United States upward of $2 billion per week, and the price tag is likely to top what was spent on the Vietnam War.

Perhaps the "shock and awe" necessary to bring about regime change would have served the American national interest if (1) the invasion had been supported by international law and an international coalition of forces, (2) the dictatorship of Saddam Hussein had posed a genuine threat to the United States, (3) the action had genuinely furthered the assault on terrorism, (4) the American citizenry had been able to deliberate meaningfully on the legitimacy of military action, (5) the military action had improved the international standing of the United States, or (6) there had been any real prospect of forming a genuine democracy in Iraq. It has become clear, however, that none of these conditions pertained.

Three justifications exist under international law for regime change. The first is to avert a humanitarian catastrophe, and no one has suggested that a humanitarian catastrophe was on the agenda in Iraq; in fact, the worst humanitarian catastrophes perpetrated by the regime of Saddam Hussein occurred while the United States was supporting him in his disastrous war with Iran. The second justification for regime change is self-defense. Since it was not Saddam who attacked the United States, but the other way around, this justification would require proof that weapons of mass destruction were being hoarded by Saddam and that Iraq would constitute a genuine threat to the United States. In his State of the Union speech of January 2003, President Bush insisted that Saddam possessed twenty-six thousand liters of anthrax; thirty-eight thousand liters of botulinum toxin; one million pounds of sarin, mustard, and VX nerve gas; thirty thousand munitions for delivery; mobile biological weapons laboratories; and uranium from Niger.

None of this was ever found.[15] But even if there had been an authentic belief that these weapons actually existed,[16] the preemptive strike undertaken against Iraq still would have contravened international law. In Iraq, unlike in Afghanistan, the UN Security Council never sanctioned military action—which speaks to the third legal justification for regime change. The pathetic performance by Secretary of State Colin Powell at the United Nations, where he tried to substantiate the existence of weapons of mass destruction by means of misinformation and unverified claims, tainted any meaningful discourse that might have taken place. His speech initiated the erosion of sympathy accorded the United States in the aftermath of 9/11 and the collapse of its moral standing everywhere in the world.

Declassified reports of the Senate Select Committee on Intelligence also suggest that, despite Bush administration claims, there were no links between Saddam Hussein and al Qaeda.[17] There is now little doubt that exiled Iraqis such as Ahmad Chalabi purposely misinformed both their neoconservative allies in the White House and credulous journalists such as Judith Miller of the *New York Times*, not only about the weapons possessed by Saddam Hussein and the connections between his regime and terrorist organizations but also about the greeting that the liberation of Iraq would receive from its citizenry.[18] The United States was taken for a ride by Vice President Dick Cheney, Ambassador to the United Nations John Bolton, and especially former Secretary of Defense Donald Rumsfeld and his sidekick Paul Wolfowitz, along with the others who called for Saddam's overthrow in the "Report for the New American Century of 2000." Their cynicism led them to lie, and they lied to obfuscate their incompetence and gullibility. Based on the beliefs that the war would be over quickly and that the Iraqi citizens would welcome the U.S. military, an invasion of Iraq was "inevitable" by July 2002.

The now famous Downing Street memo confirms this.[19] First published by the *Times of London* on May 1, 2005, the memo contains minutes of a meeting in which British Intelligence Chief Richard Dearlove, who had just returned from the White House, told Prime Minister Tony Blair that intelligence and facts "were being fixed around the policy" and that, although the case against Saddam was "thin," military action was on the agenda. Written by British national security aide Matthew Rycroft, the memo also makes it clear that the invasion would prove "protracted and costly" and that "little thought" had been given to "the aftermath and how to shape it." It noted that since an arbitrary determination of the need for regime change contravened international law, "it was necessary to create the conditions" that would make it legal.[20]

The Downing Street memo suggests that going before the United Nations was a sham from the start. Cheney, in fact, saw it as unnecessary, but the Bush administration ceded to Blair's concern that the invasion be given an imprimatur by the United Nations. Blair apparently feared a revolt among the backbenchers of his Labour Party should Britain go to war as anything other than a last resort. In light of the Downing Street memo, however, the allies' reliance on Hans Blix and other honest weapons inspectors working for the United Nations can be construed not as an attempt to avoid war but rather as an incompetent attempt to trap Saddam. Precisely because Iraq had no weapons of mass destruction, Bush and Blair believed that Saddam's inability to produce and then eliminate them could be used as a justification for war.

Another tactic complemented this one. In the *Sunday Times* of May 29, 2005, Michael Smith reported that the Royal Air Force and American aircraft had doubled the rate at which they were dropping bombs on Iraq in 2002 to provoke Saddam Hussein into giving the allies another excuse for war. By August, in fact, Smith noted that it was already possible to speak of a "full air offensive." The Downing Street memo references claims that napalm-like bombs had been used by the American military.[21] Perhaps even more devastating, however, are the statements that the war actually began before the official attack of March 2003, before congressional authorization of the war in October 2002, and before the November UN resolution that would send inspectors into Iraq.[22]

At a hearing dealing with the Downing Street memo organized by John Conyers (D-Mich.) before the House Judiciary Committee in June 2005, calls were finally heard for the impeachment of the president. On December 20, 2005, the House staff noted that there was a prima facie case that the president, vice president, and other important members of the Bush administration had committed a number of federal crimes, including fraud against the United States, making false statements to Congress, violating the War Powers Resolution, misusing federal funds, torture, retaliating against witnesses and other individuals, and misusing intelligence information. In this regard, it is relevant to point to the Bush administration's connections to the Enron scandal, the leaking of information that "outed" CIA veteran Valerie Plame and destroyed her career, and the surveillance of American citizens. And while on the subject of the CIA, a report completed in May 2005 noted that Iraq was producing a "new breed" of Islamic jihadists who could go on to destabilize other countries.[23] Another report, based on information culled by sixteen intelligence agencies, suggested that the Iraq war has sparked an increase in both Islamic fundamentalism and terrorism throughout the world.[24]

But the Downing Street memo remains the smoking gun.[25] It confirms that President Bush and his neoconservative advisers lied to the American people about the threat posed by Saddam Hussein and manipulated information that would lead public opinion to support the war. The only serious justification for the invasion of Iraq would have been proof that Saddam's regime was somehow linked with Osama bin Laden and al

Qaeda. But notes taken in the immediate aftermath of 9/11 by aides of Secretary of Defense Rumsfeld had him stating: "Hard to get good case. Need to move swiftly. . . . Near term target needs—go massive—sweep it all up, things related and not."[26] Secretary of State Powell also admitted that there was no proof of a link between Saddam Hussein and al Qaeda, and his former aide Lawrence Wilkerson stated that a "Cheney-Rumsfeld cabal" was running American foreign policy.

Democracy has been trumpeted as a product of the Iraq war. That a vicious dictatorship has fallen from power, elections have taken place, and a constitution is being drafted might yet prove to be important developments along the democratic path. But for the moment, they remain small steps. It is the height of misguided optimism to suggest that Iraq is now a sovereign state with a regime that commands loyalty from its citizens. Intolerance has grown since the toppling of Saddam, paramilitary organizations have multiplied, the elections proved fraudulent, and the constitution is actually more like a peace treaty among the groups that control the three regions of Iraq: the Kurds, the Shiites, and the Sunnis.[27] The new state has already been radically decentralized, and the influence of the national government is minimal when it comes to the role of Islamic law, the standing of women, and the distribution of oil profits.

The existence of a constitution does not tell the whole story. It should be remembered that Saddam ran a society in which 80 percent of Iraqis were employed by the government. Attempts were made to "liberalize" the economy in the wake of the American invasion, but these only whetted the appetites of foreign investors close to the U.S. government, such as Bechtel and Halliburton, for the entire wealth of Iraq. The current government of Iraq is, by contrast, committed to employing the state to foster economic equity. But between 60 and 70 percent of Iraqis are now unemployed in various areas of the country, and this is before taking into consideration the future impact of a devastated infrastructure on education, health, and investment and how the explosion in crime will affect the resumption of normal life. The dinar is virtually worthless, and, according to Felah Alwan, who heads the Federation of Workers' Councils and Unions of Iraq, agricultural workers receive less than $70 a month. Most people in the villages work for $1 a day, and even on construction sites around Baghdad and Nasariya, workers receive only about $4 a day. Oil production is now well below prewar levels, and more than $11 billion worth of oil revenue has been lost. Ninety-two percent of Baghdad households have an unstable supply of electricity, 39 percent have no safe drinking water, and 25 percent of children under the age of five suffer from malnutrition.

Resurrecting the economy will require huge infusions of capital, or extraordinary austerity with respect to benefits accorded workers, and it remains unclear either how to garner the former or how to bring about the latter. The bureaucracy is a wreck, and the only people with inner knowledge of its workings are civil servants of the former regime. Most of them are Sunnis—a minority that held power under Saddam—and they tend to view the present government as an occupation of Kurds and Shiites. There are few incentives for the Sunnis to strengthen a new nation in which ethnic and ideological groups that they perceive as enemies will prevail. The new federal government will certainly not give primacy to their concerns. In addition, a civil war is crosscutting the insurgency directed at the existing constitutional regime. As long as the Shiites constitute a majority and receive support from Iran, and as long as the Kurds retain a strong paramilitary organization and are intent on autonomy, the Sunnis will remain a social minority, their interpretation of Islam will receive secondary status, and their political influence will be tempered. Thus, in spite of the

Sunnis' participation in the first Iraqi elections, there are obvious reasons for them to support the insurgency.

The fundamental contradiction defining Iraqi democracy remains what it has been since the fall of Saddam: a new constitutional assembly has claimed legitimacy even though its ability to rule rests on the support of an occupying power. The only way the new constitutional democracy can present itself as sovereign is for the occupying power to leave. If the United States leaves, however, Iraq might plunge even deeper into civil war. No reference to a repressed civic culture of democracy or the supposed yearning for Western democracy can change this situation, and no reliance on political finesse to divide the rebels can alter this reality. All other issues ultimately derive from the frailty of the new regime and its dependence on the United States. These issues include the utter devastation of the country; the deep rifts among the Sunnis, Shiites, and Kurds; an insurgency that has turned everyday life into a shambles; and the exodus of the middle class. Iraq has become the most dangerous place on earth—not merely for the soldiers of the occupying power but also for the citizens forced to endure the descent into civil war.

The most basic criterion of sovereignty, according to a political tradition that goes back to Machiavelli, is a state's ability to hold a monopoly on the means of coercion. As things now stand, however, the Iraqi government has countenanced the legitimacy of roughly six private, ethnic, sectarian militias. Even the most cursory glance at the history of private militias shows that they are ideologically rigid and antidemocratic; they almost always tend to identify the national interest with their own. Trying to fold them into the regular armed forces would be like putting the fox in charge of the chicken coop.

Shiite and Kurdish militias are already engaging in kidnappings, assassinations, and acts of violence throughout southern

Iraq and setting up independent and unaccountable areas of authority.[28] Intent on controlling the city of Kirkuk and envisioning a Kurdish state, that militia is now openly policing a region that had already gained a measure of autonomy under Saddam Hussein. The Kurdish *pesh merga* is composed of roughly 100,000 partisans; the Shiite militia, known as the Badr Organization, is not much smaller. In contrast, the government's Special Commandos Force has only 10,000 members, and it has been notably ineffective in preventing the assassinations of numerous Sunni dignitaries. All the major leaders of all the major factions in Iraq are connected with the leadership of paramilitary organizations.

As a consequence, although all the groups may have a stake in opposing the insurgency, none of them has a stake in allowing the new state to retain a monopoly on the means of coercion. The new constitution has papered over the most telling questions facing the new state and has divided central and regional authority in ways that satisfy no major group. The Shiite clergy has received various privileges at the expense of the government, and Islam is treated not as simply one source of legislative legitimacy but rather as its primary inspiration. Islamic law, or sharia, will clearly undermine women's rights and have a sharp impact on civil liberties, divorce, inheritance, and the private sphere of social life. Terrorism against Iraqi civilians is continuing unabated, and towns that were once considered purged of insurgents, such as Falluja, have seen the resistance rise again from the ashes. What remains is only the dead letter of a "constitution."

The American occupation of Iraq has eroded the belief in Western democratic values and the standing of the United States in the world community. Scandalized by a pattern of torture that extends beyond the Middle East, 75 percent of Iraqi citizens—97 percent of Sunnis, 82 percent of Shiites, and

41 percent of Kurds—believe that the presence of American troops is actually fueling the insurgency.[29] The major Shiite and Sunni parties have all recognized this fact and have publicly asked for the Americans' withdrawal. In the United States, meanwhile, the vision of an oil-rich, self-sufficient, secular democracy with a reconstructed infrastructure has gone the way of all flesh.[30] Striking is the lack of genuine self-criticism by the entire political establishment. Hardly any major supporters of the war from either party have been willing to reflect on the assumptions that got the United States into this mess in the first place or on the legitimate opposition that the invasion generated throughout the world.

What comes next is anybody's guess: a weak democracy with a legitimacy deficit, a partition of Iraq, or a new dictatorship. Regarding the democratic legitimacy of the current regime, it rests on little more than the absence of Saddam Hussein. So long as ethnic or religious leaders exert control over private militias, Iraqi politics—to the extent that it remains civil—will increasingly turn into bargaining based on military calculation. A partitioning of Iraq among Sunnis, Kurds, and Shiites remains a genuine possibility. What kind of regimes would emerge is unclear, although it is doubtful that any of them would be particularly tolerant of outsiders and dissidents. Finally, should Iraq remain united, it is likely that the strongest of its warlords would survive in coalition with weaker adversarial allies. Whether the United States stays or whether it goes, a new strongman (with or without a mustache) is probably already peeking out from the shadows, concerned only with assuming power and formulating an ideology—whether secular or theocratic—that can justify its solitary exercise.

The invasion of Iraq was a catastrophic—and predictable—mistake from the start. Those who once favored it now bandy about the idea that turning the country over to the Iraqis immediately after the invasion would have saved the situation. But while seeking to shift the blame, they forget that the new Iraqi government never had any legitimacy. It also lacked an army, a police force, and a functioning bureaucracy; its American-sponsored leaders, such as Ahmad Chalabi, had no support whatsoever among the masses. As for the argument that more military force should have been used, and more resources committed, one need only count the corpses and dream of what could have been done with the more than $1 trillion already wasted on this barbarous enterprise.

There can be little doubt that the hegemony exerted by neoconservatives over U.S. foreign policy is at an end. Old foreign policy hands from the Reagan administration and that of the elder Bush, brought together in a commission called the Iraq Study Group headed by James Baker, were already searching for an alternative before the congressional elections in 2006. Nevertheless, they were faced with an intractable reality: American intervention had made any reasonably positive "solution" wishful thinking. They had few options. The belief that Jordan or Saudi Arabia or any other Islamic state would be willing to enter the fray and gradually substitute their forces for those of the United States—even while other members of the "coalition of the willing" were frantically pulling out—was utopian. The United States might have sought to engage Iran and Syria in a diplomatic effort to end those two nations' support for the insurgency in Iraq. But that would have required a very different perspective on foreign policy. As things now stand in 2007, Iran has stated its intention to open three banks in Iraq that would serve the purposes of reconstruction, while President Bush has decided upon a "surge" strategy that would bring 20,000 more American troops into Iraq to stabilize the existing regime. But the call for a surge, rather than serving the national interest, was a last desperate attempt to save the legacy of a despicable administration. The U.S. Congress offered nonbinding resolutions condemning the new escalation and, in an attempt to make the inevitable more palatable, suggested "timetables" for withdrawal. With every day that the United States has remained in Iraq, however, conditions have only gotten worse. There is no reason to believe that this judgment is subject to change. It is long past time to admit that this war, which should never have been fought, is irretrievably lost. Only one strategy remains for Americans who really want to "support the troops"—immediate withdrawal.

4

Twilight in Tehran

My last trip to Iran was in September 2005. I had traveled through parts of the country in 2003 after participating in the Second International Human Rights Conference at Mofid University in Qom, but I was thrilled at the thought of again visiting the ruins of Persepolis and the cities of Esfahan, Shiraz, and Yazd. I was part of U.S. Academics for Peace, an independent delegation of twelve academic groups from various universities that was led by the indefatigable Dr. James Jennings and sponsored by Conscience International. Some of us had been in Baghdad with Jennings as part of another delegation a few months before the American invasion of Iraq. Our concern this time was the possibility of a preemptive strike by the United States or Israel against Iran, but we did not experience the same sense of urgency in Tehran that we had in Baghdad. We knew that the Iraq war had weakened Americans' will to engage in yet another war, that the U.S. military was already stretched thin, and that Hurricane Katrina combined with our military adventures abroad had made the cost of yet another preemptive strike prohibitive to the rational mind. As of 2007, however, the propaganda machine was still being revved up, the right-wing talk media was still demanding "action," and what had been termed the "neoconservative cabal" led by Vice President Dick Cheney was still raring to go. One never knows what will happen when the rhetoric gets hot: sometimes the losers are most prone to gamble everything on one last spin of the roulette wheel.

Our visit occurred during the time when Mahmoud Ahmadinejad, a relatively unknown religious populist leader, won the presidency of Iran. We sensed a disillusionment with and general anger over the corruption and ineffectiveness that had held sway during the presidency of Mohammed Khatami. In restaurants and teahouses we listened to jokes about him and his cronies, as well as people's hopes for his successor. The desire for change was in the air. Everyday people were calling for a reinvigoration of the moral and religious legacy of the Ayatollah Khomeini, and we visited the huge and fantastic mosque complex being built in his memory on the outskirts of Tehran. It was the time when Iran began trumpeting its nuclear program for domestic energy, which might yet produce a nuclear device (although such a development is years away).[1] As with many nations in the Middle East, Iran was experiencing a revival of the religious identity that had been so intense in the 1980s. National self-determination was combining with contempt for what was seen as the double standard on nuclear technology imposed by Western nations, Israeli policy in the Occupied Territories, the invasion of Iraq, and U.S. control over Afghanistan.

Our group reached the conclusion that authoritarian trends would only be strengthened by the threat of sanctions and possible attack. That has indeed been the case: on August 8, 2006, the Center for the Protection of Human Rights, led by Shirin Ebadi (who received the Nobel Peace Prize in 2003), was banned by the government. Since then, universities have come under increasing pressure, newspapers and magazines have been closed, and various intellectuals have been jailed.[2] But still, Iran retains democratic elements: Ahmadinejad can, in principle, be voted out of office. Besides, for the United

States to contemplate military action now because of what *might* happen years down the road runs against every tenet of political realism.

Modernity and tradition confront each other everywhere in the Middle East. In Iran, however, the international repercussions of the domestic conflict between these two forces have been particularly severe. Western nations have been looking with increasing suspicion on Iran's decision to build a nuclear reactor in Natanz, about an hour's drive from the beautiful city of Esfahan, with its marvelous square and its spectacular blue Lotfollah mosque. Contemptuous of suggestions that the most likely beneficiary of external interference in Iran would be the proponents of a populist form of religious nationalism, the United States and Israel, as usual, have been the most unyielding in their condemnation of its nuclear policy. Not satisfied with the disaster they have created in Iraq, neoconservatives have been calling for regime change in Iran. Even before the invasion of Lebanon, moreover, Israeli officials were warning that they could not wait for the conclusion of negotiations and that an aerial strike on Natanz was a distinct possibility. Especially in the United States, the propaganda machine was working overtime. Iraq had taught us what Bush and the boys were capable of doing. Leaders of states such as Iran and Syria were naturally forced to assume the pessimistic rather than the optimistic outcome of a crisis. Arguably, only the staggering incompetence shown by the Bush administration in dealing with the insurgency in Iraq and the hurricanes at home had saved Iran and Syria from suffering the fate of their neighbor.

The goals of our delegation were clear: we wanted to spread a message of peace, build intercultural exchanges, offer some insights into the United States under the rule of Bush, and learn more about the policies and culture of those nations living under the threat of war. We sensed the strong traces of anti-Semitism, but we knew little about the country's new president and, like the Iranians we met, we were not yet ready to make any judgments. Most of us recognized, however, the connection between mounting foreign threats and increasing domestic trends toward authoritarianism and religious xenophobia in the Middle East. Thus, we were fearful of what might come to pass.

Identified with the Ayatollah Khomeini, the hostage crisis of 1979, and the revolutionary posters and graffiti proclaiming "Death of America" and "Down with the Great Satan," Iran now appears in the American popular imagination as perhaps the most dangerous member of the original "axis of evil." It is. Its ties with Syria are close, and Iran has been a staunch supporter of Hezbollah in Lebanon and Hamas in Palestine. This is incendiary, to say the least. And, given the $1 billion in economic aid it supplies to the Shiites and Kurds in Iraq, Iran now wields great influence on the Supreme Council for the Islamic Revolution,[3] the largest political party in that occupied nation. Turning an independent Iran into the dominant power in the region was, ironically, among the most important unintended consequences of the Iraq war.[4] In fact, this outcome was what U.S. foreign policy in the region had long sought to avoid. Maintaining Tehran as an ally and preventing it from "going communist" was the principal purpose behind American involvement in the overthrow of Mossadegh in 1953 in favor of Shah Pahlavi.[5] Keeping Iran weak, meanwhile, was the obvious reason why the United States and most of Europe had supported Saddam Hussein in his long and bloody war with his neighbor.

More than preventing the spread of "terrorism" is involved in understanding the current crisis spawned by a mixture of U.S. foreign policy and Iran's decision to build a nuclear reactor.

Iran was never a European colony, but its politics were long dominated by Britain, Russia, and the United States. There is also a long-standing distrust of Iran and its claims to national self-determination by the West in general and the United States in particular.[6] This distrust has now been transformed into a self-fulfilling prophecy. The host of new U.S. military bases located in Afghanistan, Turkey, and Iraq were created largely due to the fear that Iran would use its exceptional geopolitical position and new stature to further Islamic extremism and stage an attack on Israel. Feeling itself surrounded, Iran reacted by calling for the elimination of Israel and worse, along with a new and radically anti-Western foreign policy. The disastrous Iraq policy pursued by the United States surely emboldened the current regime in Tehran. It generated precisely the kind of anti-Western paranoia that puts liberals and moderates increasingly at risk.

As in so much of the Middle East, external pressure has tilted the domestic scale in Iran toward authoritarianism rather than democracy.[7] That remains the case. Little meaningful dialogue with the Islamic Republic of Iran has been undertaken. Instead, the United States has sought to destabilize its avowed enemy.[8] There has, since the spring of 2006, been constant talk of a military attack against Iran staged by either the United States or Israel or both.[9] Ongoing attempts by President Bush to humiliate Iran, brand it as a rogue state, and present it as a nuclear threat to U.S. security appear to be a replay of the propaganda wave that preceded the invasion of Iraq. It has also intensified the attraction of Islam, fostered a sense of isolation, generated a more authoritarian-religious trend in the state, and engendered a fervid commitment to national self-determination within Iranian society. The policy originally pursued by Western states and pushed particularly hard by the Bush administration has produced heightened tensions, domestic paranoia, populist fanaticism, and the possibility of yet another military adventure that will lead to the trench and then to the morgue.

Both the Iranian leadership's seemingly unyielding insistence on building a nuclear reactor and the recent electoral losses by the more Western and reformist elements of Iranian society have been framed by paranoid anti-Semitism and an obsessive preoccupation with self-determination by a nation under siege. Therefore, it is useful to consider not only the usual arguments against nuclear energy—Chernobyl, it should be noted, is not that far from Tehran—but also the unique stresses that the current nuclear policy has placed on the citizenry. Iran has seen its stock market plunge 30 percent since September 2005. The threat of international economic sanctions is real should Iran be dragged in front of the UN Security Council. Making public the decision to build a reactor has arguably put Iran in the position of lacking a genuine deterrent to Israeli or American aggression while apparently planning an attack on the United States sometime in the near future.

National self-determination, the wish to stand up against the imperialists, trumps the seemingly objective and material definition of the national interest. That is why Iran has attempted to frame its demand for nuclear energy as a universal "right," kept the construction of its nuclear facilities within the terms required by the nonproliferation treaty, and—unlike the United States—signed the additional protocol, with its provision for snap inspections. Iran also for a time allowed the installation of cameras by the International Atomic Energy Agency (IAEA) to supervise its nuclear work and has undergone the most intrusive inspections of any member of the United Nations. Throughout the debate, Iran has claimed that its intention is to produce nuclear energy for peaceful purposes, and there is no hard evidence to suggest the opposite.[10] Even if Iran were building a nuclear bomb, according to a national intelligence estimate, such a device would not be ready until the early or middle years of the next decade, and creating a delivery system capable of attacking the United States would take much longer.[11]

Only Israel and the United States have disagreed with these predictions, and only these countries have claimed that Iran poses an imminent danger that might require preemptive action. Imagining a joint military operation against Iran by Israel and the United States does not stretch the limits of reason. In the first half of 2005, Vice President Dick Cheney stated that Iran was "right at the top of the list" when it came to rogue states, and he speculated that Israel could "be doing the bombing for us" without any American pressure being applied.[12] Secretary of State Condoleezza Rice has, in the same vein, told the world that the United States cannot wait forever for diplomacy to do its job, while Richard Perle and his clique remain intent on "liberating" yet another country. Unleashing the ideology of the preemptive strike to justify American actions in Iraq has, however, backfired; it has created an incentive for nations that feel threatened by the West to build nuclear weapons for defense and use them as a form of what Richard Haass, president of the Council on Foreign Relations, has termed "symbolic currency."

Working toward the abolition or, at least, nonproliferation of nuclear weapons seemingly demands a policy predicated on reducing the value of this symbolic currency. But that is apparently not the position of the Bush administration. Refusing to even consider cutting its own arsenal of eight thousand nuclear weapons, the United States is unconcerned with the dramatic imbalance between its nuclear might and that of all other nations. Its leaders take the position that they have the wisdom to decide which nations are responsible enough to have the bomb

(India, Pakistan, and Israel) and which are not (Iran). Unwilling to discuss why Iran should not have what Western nations and other onetime "rogue" states such as China and Russia possess, the Bush administration has no specific plan for action other than the employment of military threats, economic sanctions, and international isolation of a major power.

Iran is surrounded by nuclear powers: Russia, Pakistan, India, and Israel. The United States has occupied Iraq and is threatening Syria. Given the historical interference in the area by Western powers in general and the United States in particular, mistrust if not hyperparanoia on the part of the Iranian leadership is understandable.[13] Once the UN Security Council decided on sanctions against Iran, it was to be expected that on-site inspections would be blocked.[14] The Iranian leadership can still claim that it asked for nothing not specifically guaranteed to the signatories of the nonproliferation treaty, which was signed by the United States, and that the Bush administration's demands fall outside the framework of that document and thus have no legal or ethical basis. The "crisis" sparked by the Iranian pursuit of nuclear energy may actually be a red herring, since the real threat today is not a missile but a bomb smuggled into an urban center in a briefcase. In any event, perhaps the best way to deal with a rogue state is by integrating it into the world community rather than excluding it, emphasizing the need for regime change, or bombing it to smithereens.

Other tendencies besides hypernationalism, anti-Semitism, and religious extremism exist in Iran, and these require cultivation. Iran's major writer, the fourteenth-century poet Hafez, was a giant of world literature but is virtually unknown in the West, other than to those who have read Goethe's *West-Oestliche Divan*. Iran also possesses a cultural heritage that reaches back past Cyrus the Great to the fabled religious figure Zoroaster, but this is largely ignored. Our delegation was reminded of all this during a trip to the Iran National Museum, where we saw the "laughing lion" from 1250 B.C., which any modernist would have been proud to produce, and the remains of the "salt man" from 1700 B.C., found in a salt mine where he was probably murdered—his leg stuffed in a boot, remnants of his clothes, and a golden earring enmeshed in some hair curled around what was left of his skull. We saw the life-size sculpture of a calf and beautiful renditions of cats, as well as detailed engravings, seals, multicolored vases, and plates dating from 5000 B.C. We also thought about how much President Bush and his boys cared about the treasures of Iraq.[15]

Time means something different in the Middle East. In the United States we are amazed at artifacts that are a few hundred years old; in Europe, such treasures might be a thousand years old. In the Middle East things do not get interesting until they are a few thousand years old. Humbling is the simple and dignified tomb of Cyrus the Great, and awe-inspiring are the tombs of his descendants—Darius, Xerxes, Artaxerxes—that were carved into the huge rock of Naqsh-e-Rustam. Most fantastic, however, is what remains of Persepolis, with its Gate of all Nations and the Aramaic, Babylonian, and Edomite inscriptions above it. Persepolis, built in 580 B.C. by artisans brought to Persia from everywhere in the known world, is the first and arguably the greatest example of cosmopolitan architecture. Now, of course, it is only ruins. Gone are the colors that once adorned the columns and the houses; gone are the faces from the friezes that were obliterated and disfigured by Islamic fanatics; gone are the gardens known as the *parades,* from which the word *paradise* derives. Alexander the Great—a general from the West—destroyed Persepolis. Legend has it that he commanded his troops to perform this act on the dare of a mistress. More likely, the deed was done to strike at the heart of the Persian empire. Persepolis, among the greatest cultural treasures of humanity, can be considered an early example of "collateral damage"—and might prove to be once again.

Cultural ignorance breeds political ignorance. Iran retains a tradition of national independence that goes back thousands of years and a religious orthodoxy that stems from the victory of Islam over what had become an increasingly corrupt and hyperritualized Zoroastrianism in the ninth century. But it also evidences a tradition of liberal tolerance and cosmopolitanism that reaches back through the creation of a constitution and a parliament in 1906 to the Savyed Renaissance of the nineteenth century to Hafez and ultimately to Cyrus the Great, who allowed the Jews to rebuild their Temple and his other subjects to worship as they chose. Some like to say that this fundamental division is reflected today in the cosmopolitan style of Shiraz and Tehran versus the somber orthodoxy and gray provincialism of a city like Qom. In any event, these tendencies manifest themselves in the Iranian republic, with its conflict between a liberal—or better, moderate—Islamic political constituency and another that is more orthodox and authoritarian.

Forgotten is that, even in the present Islamic Republic of Iran, elections between competing candidates take place, and civil liberties exist within certain fixed parameters. Especially with regard to women, however, the Western notion of rights lacks the kind of overriding consensus in Iran that exists elsewhere. The Koran casts a long shadow, and even reformist movements remain profoundly influenced by Islam. Ahmadinejad is contemplating introducing a new dress code that would ban Western fashions, even as he is contemplating armbands for Jews and Christians. Resistance against the regime is growing from within: students are demonstrating, intellectuals are trying to find a voice, and economic hardship is fueling resentment. There is an opportunity to offer an alternative to Ahmadinejad in the next election. But that will not occur if a bellicose policy from the outside is seen as justifying his rantings. Trying to engage in regime change would also be a disaster. Whatever the criticisms of the regime, Iranian citizens are united in their allegiance to the Islamic republic, and, no less than in Iraq, their resistance against an invader would be fierce.

Western leaders and analysts have generally identified reformism with a dull pragmatism that elides issues pertaining to religion. Such was the position defining the followers of former president Mohammed Khatami in the last election. They sought to temper many domestic ideological excesses hanging over from the time of the Ayatollah Khomeini, and in terms of foreign affairs, they called for a "dialogue of civilizations." Khatami proudly told our group that he had reduced the number of ritual stonings of individuals for various crimes, including adultery, from twenty-six to one (really two). But the reformist agenda did not go very far with regard to fostering institutional accountability. Its proponents opposed what are usually considered the "extremists." Furious that the highest court had obstructed their legislative agenda, and acting in accordance with the will of conservative mullahs, the reformers threatened to walk out of parliament. But, when push came to shove, they recanted. The reformers also oversaw a spurt in national economic growth from which urban and agricultural workers did not benefit. No less than the mullahs, whom many Iranians privately condemn as thieves, careerist reformers benefited from a palpable increase in corruption. Their leader, Khatami, neither exudes charisma nor inspires confidence. Chubby-cheeked and dressed in religious garb, unctuous and careful with every word, he tried to appear urbane but came off as slick. After an audience of about an hour, our delegation realized that not a single question had been answered. I understood why so many everyday people we met blamed him and his followers for the deep malaise and why they dreamed of the heady days surrounding the Revolution of 1979 led by the Ayatollah Khomeini.[16] Indeed, this kind of nostalgia helped produce the presidential victory of Mahmoud Ahmadinejad.

Western media and the "experts" were astonished. Ahmadinejad was seen as coming out of nowhere. But the Iranians did not see him as a dark horse. He had served as the wildly popular mayor of Tehran and then governor of the largest province in the country. Ahmadinejad was an activist during the hostage crisis, an important participant in the revolution, and an avowed critic of Western policies in the region. The citizenry was aware that Iran was in a perilous geopolitical situation caused by the creation of American bases in Afghanistan and Iraq following the "liberation" of those countries. Ahmadinejad's campaign was based on three planks: share the oil profits more equitably, crack down on corruption among the mullahs, and lift the malaise that had fallen over the land. A young journalist I met said that the words of Ahmadinejad touched the heart, while those of Khatami and the rest were only words.[17] It is always dangerous in politics to rely on the heart.

Ahmadinejad daringly mixed religious, international, and national themes. He presented himself as devout but distanced from the establishmentarian mullahs. It now appears that Iran will endure new forms of cultural repression to prepare the country for the reappearance of the hundred-year-old "hidden imam."[18] Ahmadinejad embraced the nuclear issue to foster national enthusiasm even while, in keeping with the utopian vision of a unified caliphate spanning the Muslim world, calling for an economic union of all Islamic states. He has also forged what might be termed an Eastern strategy in foreign affairs. Iran has negotiated a new alliance with Syria that is important to the United States insofar as both nations exert influence over Hamas and Hezbollah and have a stake in Iraq. A new crescent of unity is looming, which the United

States might shatter by reaching a deal with Iran, even while China is becoming a primary trading partner and Russia has agreed to sell Iran antiaircraft missiles as part of a $1 billion arms deal. President Ahmadinejad is undoubtedly also aware that a boycott of Iranian oil would result in oil prices going through the roof. He has consolidated his grip by seeking to infuse everyday life with a new religiosity—banning Western music is just one example of this tendency—while ranting about the need to wipe Israel off the map. He has also pushed the envelope further by stating publicly that Iran will build heavy water facilities and numerous nuclear reactors to increase electricity. Ahmadinejad's themes have all highlighted traditional opposition to Western hegemony, the right to national self-determination, and the tone of Ayatollah Khomeini and the Revolution of 1979.

The "quiet revolution" that was once considered the hope of liberal forces is turning into a nightmare. Crackdowns on dissidents and individual liberty are occurring with increasing rapidity, justified by "national security." Tehran University now has a cleric as its president, dozens of professors have been forced into retirement, radical students have been imprisoned, the national bureaucracy is being whipped into shape, and—in line with fascist governments of the past—contempt for human rights was openly expressed by sending Saeed Mortazavi, a feared public prosecutor known as "the butcher of the press," to serve as a member of Iran's delegation to the new United Nations Human Rights Council.[19] Religious fundamentalism is entering everyday life in a radical fashion, the state is merging with the mosque, the public opportunities for women have diminished, and "pragmatists" are increasingly decried as stooges of the West. Israel has become less an imperialist state than a scapegoat—the source of everything evil in the region. The critique of Israeli policies is turning into a rather conspiratorial variant of anti-Semitism as the call for international Islamic unity is merging with a xenophobic and paranoid nationalism.

None of this can possibly sit well with decent people anywhere. But the decision to engage in military action is fraught with obstacles.[20] The Iraqi debacle, indeed, should have taught the United States to recognize practical constraints and the moral limits of possible action. Putting together an international coalition would prove virtually impossible, and the attempt would create rifts with trading partners of Iraq like Russia, China, India, and Pakistan. Tehran has twelve million inhabitants, whereas Baghdad had seven million, and there is national support for the legacy of the Ayatollah Khomeini and the Islamic republic that did not exist for Saddam and his regime in Iraq. Iran is also more powerful militarily than Iraq ever was, and it is conceivable that an attack by the United States would result in thousands of volunteers crossing the border.[21] In this vein, because precision air strikes would allow the Islamic republic too many retaliatory options, some U.S. military planners argue that any attack on Iran must involve more than merely the bombing of the nuclear site at Natanz.[22] There is also a good chance that Iran would close down the Strait of Hormuz following an attack on its nuclear facilities. As a major oil producer, it is capable of manipulating already high prices worldwide. Iran also has decisive influence over Hezbollah and other terrorist groups, so that the possibility of new attacks against civilian targets in Israel and the West might increase dramatically following military intervention.[23] A U.S. assault on Iran would, following Iraq, obviously appear to be an attack on the Islamic world. In addition, U.S. forces are already stretched thin, reconstruction in the face of Hurricane Katrina will cost hundreds of billions of dollars, the price of the Iraq war keeps growing, and Americans are sick of war.

But there are some who still insist that the military option should be chosen. Conservative organizations such as the American Enterprise Institute, as well as Zionist lobbyists and think tanks such as the American Israeli Public Affairs Committee (AIPAC) and the Jewish Institute for National Security Affairs (JINSA), have called for regime change in Iran. They believe that a "clash of civilizations" is inevitable and that it should take place sooner rather than later. Regime change, in their view, would pave the way for a victory of liberal forces, and contingency plans for bringing it about are already being developed. Former prime minister Benjamin Netanyahu, now the scion of the Far Right in Israeli politics, has already said publicly that he would back a preemptive strike against Iran. Vice President Cheney and former Ambassador to the United Nations John Bolton, both staunch neoconservatives and one-time members of JINSA, have insisted that the UN Security Council's refusal to deal sternly with Iran means that handling the nuclear crisis will be left to the United States.[24] There is also much talk of pressure being exerted by the United States and Great Britain on the IAEA to overrule its own inspectors and declare that Iran has breached the nonproliferation treaty.

Certain extreme neoconservative factions in the Bush administration undoubtedly believe that yet another appropriately justified foreign intervention can reinvigorate a disintegrating sense of unity and nationalism in the United States. These factions show an ever-growing desire to blame the catastrophic failures of their own policies in Iraq on an outside force. At the annual convention of AIPAC, Bolton stated that Iran constitutes a "comprehensive threat" and that the "longer we wait . . . the harder it will become to solve [the crisis]." He called for the United States to use "all tools at our disposal" to prevent Iran from developing nuclear weapons.[25] There is evidence that Iran has already been bombed along its borders with Iraq, and the remains of an American spy plane have been discovered inside its territory.[26] Reports from Germany suggest that the Bush administration has prepared its allies for a possible attack on the nuclear complex in Iran. Former CIA director Porter Goss is said to have asked Turkish prime minister Recep Tayyip Erdogan for strategic support in case of an American air strike in exchange for a "green light" to attack camps of the separatist Kurdistan Workers' Party in Iran. Saudi Arabia, Jordan, and Oman have apparently been informed about U.S. plans for this "possible option."[27]

Out of sheer desperation, given Iran's new power in Iraq, the United States has stated its willingness both to endorse a UN resolution that rejects the use of military force to resolve the conflict and to engage in direct talks with President Ahmadinejad—if Iran suspends its nuclear activity. Support for that UN resolution was always halfhearted, however, and the possibility for negotiations was predicated on Iran accepting American demands before talks even began. The irony is that intransigent foreign policy pursued by Ahmadinejad is itself a desperate attempt to shore up his domestic standing following the humiliating defeat of his candidates in the elections of December 15, 2006. With inflation having risen by 20 percent and rents by 30 percent, with the economy shaken by capital flight and lack of foreign investment, the Iranian president is obviously using an inflammatory rhetoric against the United States and Israel to deflect attention from his domestic problems.[28] The question is whether the United States is willing to play into the demagogue's hands by pursuing a bellicose policy of its own that could also lead to a tragic conflagration.

With respect to the nuclear issue, the double standard employed by the United States and Europe has had a disastrous effect on policies toward Iran as well as other nations in the Middle East. The issue is not simply nuclear activity in Iran or the supposed threat it might eventually pose—should it actually produce one or two missiles—to the national security of the United States, with its vast nuclear arsenal and sophisticated defense systems. Too few in the American political mainstream consider how the rest of the world perceives the decision of the United States—the only nation to ever use a nuclear device for military purposes (not once but twice)—to support the nuclear ambitions of India and Israel yet oppose those same ambitions when expressed by Iran. The double standard only highlights what is seen as the arrogance of U.S. foreign policy and the privileges that a superpower can extend to itself. Knowledge of the double standard inflames the already ideologically charged anti-Western sentiments and strengthens the mutual misunderstanding of cultural differences and political interests. Unless that double standard is confronted, it might bring about the irrational rush to arms that progressives have consistently struggled against.

5

Syria and Its President

A Meeting with Bashar al-Assad

Syria has a particularly bad reputation in the Middle East. Authoritarian remnants of the grim and gray rule of Hafez al-Assad still hang over the country. Arbitrary incarceration and heavy censorship mark his legacy. Memories still exist of the failed military assaults on Israel and his butchering of the Islamic Brotherhood in the city of Hama in 1982. An uprising and an assassination attempt followed, leading to the deaths of twenty thousand Syrian citizens. Few saw anything other than self-interest in what amounted to Hafez al-Assad's crude attempts to control Lebanon. His long alliance with the Soviet Union was tactical, and he actually sided with Iran against his fellow Baathist Saddam Hussein in the terrible civil war of the 1980s. Hafez al-Assad showed little concern with either building a new form of Islamic republic in the manner of the Ayatollah Khomeini or fostering Pan-Arabism like Gamal Abdel Nasser of Egypt. Hafez al-Assad ruled a police state without ideological purpose or social principle. He never had a grand vision to justify his brutal exercise of power. The Baath Party, originally founded to further an Islamic socialism and anti-imperialist purposes,[1] became his personal fiefdom. Hafez al-Assad had only one concern when he died in 2000: maintaining power for himself and his family.

Thus, it was with some trepidation that our U.S. Academics for Peace delegation entered the palace of his son, Bashar al-

Assad, in Damascus for a group discussion on September 21, 2005. Educated as an ophthalmologist, Bashar had not been destined for power; his brother Basil was to have inherited the throne, but he died in an accident in 1994. We had heard that Bashar al-Assad was a weak ruler, inarticulate, and inexperienced. We encountered instead a tall man with exquisite manners, polished speech, and a sophisticated grasp of the political crises plaguing his region. Whether we agreed or disagreed with his assessments and evaluations, we all concluded that Bashar al-Assad seemed to be open to dialogue and aware of his country's perilous situation. We asked him difficult questions, and his responses were usually direct and to the point. His answers are worth considering with respect to both understanding the thinking of the Syrian elite and evaluating the prospects of an increasingly bellicose policy that has been halfheartedly embraced by most other members of the United Nations at the behest of the United States and Great Britain.

Bashar al-Assad did not shrink from the question of how he justified a "state of emergency" that had lasted for forty years and the maintenance of authoritarian rule in Syria. His answer was in some ways typical. The president of Syria initially noted that reforms to improve civil liberties had taken place under his rule. He pointed to the elimination of the infamous tribunal dealing with "crimes against the state" and the release of numerous political prisoners (two hundred more were freed in November 2005). He also emphasized the introduction of the Internet into Syrian society, and an extraordinary number of satellite television dishes were evident in the houses and housing complexes of Damascus. The president told us that his government would extend citizenship to the thousands of officially unrecognized Kurds living in Syria and that other parties would soon be able to run against the reigning Baath Party for parliamentary seats. (It should be noted that since our visit, these plans for democratic reform were suspended, although new overtures were made to Islamic supporters of the Sunni faith.)[2] Nevertheless, we realized that it would be a mistake to view the Syrian state under Bashar al-Assad as just another version of what it had been under his father or as the equivalent of Iraq under Saddam Hussein.[3]

Bashar al-Assad assuredly has blood on his hands. But he has never been a mass murderer like his father, and the rule of his family is based not merely on the secret police but also on the public sector, the bureaucracy, and a coalition of sects and ethnic groups.[4] Still, the president was adamant about the need to retain the "state of emergency" in the name of "national security." Noting the unstable situation on Syria's borders with Lebanon and Iraq, he pointed to the American double standard and asked how the United States would respond in the event of a hostile takeover of Cuba or instability in Mexico. President al-Assad was probably aware that John F. Kennedy had been ready to blow up the world in 1962 if Soviet premier Nikita Khrushchev had not backed down from his plan to install missiles in Cuba. We also knew that in Mexico and elsewhere in Central and Latin America the United States had intervened, under cover of the Monroe Doctrine, whenever "instability" seemed to exist. Every period of crisis in the history of the United States has been marked by some constriction of civil liberties.[5] Even today, the use of torture is often justified by the exigencies of war; many Americans still see Abu Ghraib as an exception rather than as part of a pattern of misconduct, and neoconservative arguments have been made to exempt Americans from international law.[6]

Of course, Syria and the United States are not the same when it comes to democracy and civil liberties. There was clearly something self-serving about the way President al-Assad justified his regime, with its state of emergency and repression of civil liberties. His government is capable of far greater repression than the relatively mild intimidation of the liberal mainstream and the mass media by the Bush administration during the invasion of Iraq. It is impossible to speak about a free press or a diversity of political views in Syria. By contrast, especially since 9/11, the principal problem in the United States revolves around what Lawrence Davidson has called the "under-utilized use of civil liberties." There is in the Western democracies the general expectation that citizens can employ civil liberties should the occasion arise. That is not the case in Syria. The double standard constantly employed by the United States is another matter, however. President al-Assad's words to that effect are echoed throughout the Middle East. Listening to his views on this matter was important, because any progressive foreign policy must ultimately begin by understanding how other nations see the Western democracies and recognizing the need for a bit of humility on the part of Western leaders when making their criticisms and exercising their power.

Bashar al-Assad made another point during our interview that touches on democracy or, better, the preconditions for its exercise. He argued that the state of emergency had to be dismantled gradually, because if an election actually took place that he lost, then the beneficiaries would be the parties championing Islamic fundamentalism. In that vein, the president invoked the example of Algeria's civil war, which claimed the lives of more than 100,000 of its citizens. Whether there is a viable democratic opposition in Syria remains an open question, and the situation in Iraq should have taught the United States and other Western nations the danger of simply assuming that such a movement exists. Indeed, according to President al-Assad, a genuinely democratic consensus is lacking in Syria. The tolerance of secularists is not matched by that of Islamic fundamentalists, who, in his view, would repress all other religious minorities should they become the majority. For this reason, the president insisted, his secular regime resting on a "state of emergency" actually allows far more cultural diversity than would a democratically elected government ruled by Islamic fundamentalists. On the streets of Damascus, secular individuals with their suits and miniskirts mingled with fundamentalists wearing religious garments. And according to the president, only with the gradual elimination of his authoritarianism could such diversity be maintained. Or, to put it another way, in the Syrian context, cultural diversity can be preserved only at the expense of political freedom. Pluralism confronts democracy. Indeed, given the resentment it produces among fundamentalists, cultural diversity also prevents the political development of a democratic consensus.

The irony is both unmistakable and unavoidable. Groups concerned with democracy and opposed to the rule of Bashar al-Assad exist. In 2005 they actually issued a joint statement, the "Damascus Declaration," which calls for lifting the forty-two-year-old emergency law, holding free elections, and releasing political prisoners. Undertaken by a coalition of secular, Kurdish, and other minority voices, with the Muslim Brotherhood in the lead—a coalition similar to the opposition against President Hosni Mubarak in Egypt—it explicitly rejected the notion that the choice for Syria is either al-Assad or Islamic extremism. Unfortunately, the document offers no clue to how strong this supposed democratic force might be, and in the Egyptian elections of November 2005, the Islamic Party constituted the majority of the opposition. President al-Assad had predicted as much.

Of course, the Syrian president's insistence on the need for a gradual rather than a radical elimination of repression and discrimination is an old ploy, and it remains, quite obviously, self-serving. Especially given that the majority of Muslims live outside the Middle East under relatively democratic regimes—in Bangladesh, India, Indonesia, and Turkey—it is not at all clear that Islamic democracy must always prove a "theo-democracy."[7] Having said that, however, most scholars would probably admit that Islamic religious law, or the sharia, is incompatible with a Western understanding of rights.[8] It remains to be determined whether a progressive strategy for the region should involve supporting moderate and relatively secular regimes as opposed to extremist and theocratic ones. Genuinely democratic movements in the Middle East have often been burned by secular authoritarian leaders (cut in the mold of Nasser), and an argument can be made that their repression of liberal critics actually drove opponents of these regimes into the arms of the Muslim Brotherhood. There is no set rule when it comes to determining which movement or leader to support in any given context. That decision must be ad hoc, based on an evaluation of the particular situation.

In any case, the critique made by Bashar al-Assad with respect to the underdevelopment of his society was striking and candid. Both the president and his wife wished to present themselves not as opponents of globalization but as modernizers in their own right. They noted with pride the gains that had been made by Syrian women, and our delegation was struck by the number of women in administrative and professorial positions at Damascus University. The first lady in particular emphasized the ongoing reforms she had initiated in the areas of spousal abuse, the rights of children, and the powers of tribal courts. Bashar al-Assad also stated frankly that in the countryside, criticizing a tribal chief might get one killed, whereas criticizing the president in particularly harsh terms would only land one in jail. Again and again, he referred to the power of tribal chieftains in the rural and less developed areas of Syria. President al-Assad stressed the strength of tribal rather than national loyalties, along with intolerant forms of Islamic fundamentalism whose appeal had only grown after the invasion of Iraq. He made it clear that this posed a threat not only to democratic reform but also to the stability of the regime. We were again made aware that the prospects for domestic reform were connected with external factors—in particular, U.S. foreign policy in the region. Since our departure, the rhetoric has been ratcheted up a notch, and a chill has fallen over whatever prospects existed for expanding civil liberties and introducing parliamentary elections.

My stay in Syria taught me some basic truths about democracy. The president left little doubt that the loosening of repressive chains depended in large part on the degree to which his regime felt threatened by outside forces. It was therefore the political regime that defined the threat—a classic instance of *raison d'etat*—as well as the response of its citizenry. Cultural expression, by the same token, comes cheaply without the possibility of political criticism. Lacking genuine civil liberties, the degree to which cultural freedom is permitted rests on the arbitrary discretion of the state and its leader. Intimidation and fear of reprisal, if not in the present then perhaps in the future, become essential to the maintenance of political order. When that thought occurred to me, I took the liberty of asking the president about the unacknowledged elephant in the room: the Hariri affair.

Rafiq Hariri, the former prime minister of Lebanon, was killed along with twenty others by a bomb blast in the middle of Beirut on February 14, 2005. The assassination followed the "cedar revolution" and the mass demonstrations that led to the withdrawal of Syrian forces from Lebanon. Syria had initially stepped in during Lebanon's horrible civil war and had supported Hezbollah's response to the Israeli invasion of 1982, when Ariel Sharon came to prominence as the "butcher of Beirut." As time passed, however, Syria gained both a political and an economic stake in the conduct of Lebanese affairs. President al-Assad insisted that Syria was never interested in annexing Lebanon; in fact, he emphasized that there was no reason for such an annexation: "it produces no oil, only trouble." In our interview with him, the president also claimed that the bulk of Syrian military forces had already been withdrawn from Lebanon by the end of 2004. When asked why Lebanon required Syria's military presence in the first place, Bashar al-Assad explained that the two nations shared the same ruling families and derived from the same tribes; if only for these reasons, he stated, "chaos in Lebanon is more dangerous to Syria than chaos in Iraq." The contradiction was glaring, and it is not surprising that President al-Assad would restate his support for Hezbollah's resistance to the Israeli invasion of Lebanon, place his own troops in a "state of alert," and be poised to take advantage of any opportunity to maximize Syrian influence on a disintegrating Lebanese state.

The motive that seems to implicate the president in the assassination of Hariri is clear enough. Although he had once been an ally of Syria, in the aftermath of the demonstrations and with the prospect of privatizing much of Lebanon, Hariri became a supporter of Lebanese national self-determination. Former Syrian vice president Abedel-Halim Khaddam supposedly heard his president threaten Hariri shortly before the assassination, but al-Assad maintained to us that he had no substantive disagreements with the Lebanese prime minister. It was not much of a defense. Hariri, after all, had come to symbolize the Lebanese quest for independence from Syria. Amid the international outcry that arose in the aftermath of his murder, his son, Saad Hariri, and the leaders of the Lebanese Druze called for an international tribunal to try those complicit in the assassination. The United Nations launched an investigation in which more than four hundred people were interviewed, sixty thousand documents were reviewed, and four high-level members of the Lebanese security apparatus were arrested.[9] Detlev Mehlis, the famous German antiterrorist prosecutor, led the investigation.

Jumping to conclusions when dealing with events in the Middle East is always hazardous. But it is hard to believe that if Syria was involved in the murder of Hariri, such an act could have been undertaken without the prior approval of President al-Assad. However, again, the president denied all responsibility for the murder, and no report ever officially stated that he was guilty of the crime or complicit in its commission. The investigation by Mehlis implicated the brother and brother-in-law of Bashar al-Assad, and the German prosecutor insisted on questioning them in Lebanon. But President al-Assad reacted swiftly: demonstrations were organized in Damascus to protest the UN report. Nor was he helpful in hastening the proceedings. Even Algeria, an otherwise close ally, demanded that Syria cooperate with Mehlis and the UN Security Council in the investigation of Hariri's death. As a consequence, although it took some time and al-Assad was accused of stalling, he skillfully agreed to a compromise. The supposed naïf decided to allow his relatives and comrades in the ruling clique to testify in Vienna, thereby preserving Syrian national sovereignty while mitigating the charge that his regime was refusing to cooperate with the investigation. In the meantime, the Syrian president continued to condemn the investigation and, in an attempt to expose what he considered the West's double standard, called on the United Nations to investigate the death of Yasir Arafat, whom many in the Middle East believe was poisoned by Israeli agents in his compound near Ramallah.

President al-Assad suggested to us that the United States and its allies had created a prejudicial climate in which Syria was already presumed guilty and that selective evidence had been assembled to confirm its guilt. His parliamentary representatives claimed that the investigation had been rigged, and they may have a point. One witness to the events apparently suggested that Bashar al-Assad was genuinely shocked when he learned that Hariri had been killed. As for the other important witnesses, one died in a car accident, and two have recanted their stories. Abu George claimed that he was offered $500,000 for his testimony. Hussam Taher Hussam, a former Syrian intelligence agent in Lebanon, has stated publicly that he was kidnapped and tortured before being offered a bribe of $1.3 million by supporters of Saad Hariri to give false testimony concerning Syrian complicity in the crime.[10] Whether any of this is true or not, the reliability of these witnesses is in doubt. In addition, the Syrian files dealing with the Hariri assassination have apparently been destroyed, and it has been suggested that members of Hussam's family were arrested and threatened by Syrian officials. Complicating the situation further was Mehlis's replacement by Serge Brammertz—a deputy prosecutor of the International Criminal Court—whose report, which focused less on the sensational narrative style and more on a highly technical examination of the Hariri murder, stated that the cooperation offered by President al-Assad was "generally satisfactory."[11] Then, too, there was the spate of bomb attacks that took place in Lebanon and the assassination of anti-Syrian journalist Gebran Tueni, editor of *An Naher,* by another car bomb. President al-Assad has insisted that the timing of this most recent murder is part of a general strategy aimed at undermining his country.[12] Indeed, judging from the bellicose statements of former UN representative John Bolton, the United States could not be more pleased at such an outcome.

With the "cartoon controversy" in Europe, the scandals surrounding the use of torture and rendition by the United States, the electoral victory of Hamas, Israel's invasion of Lebanon, and the disaster in Iraq, the Hariri affair drifted to the back pages. Bashar al-Assad appears to have averted an international crisis caused by the assassination of Hariri. But the president made repeated reference in our interview to the possibility of U.S. military action and Syria becoming another Iraq. He viewed his country as being under siege, and his fears were understandable. Even while the United Nations was accusing Syria of facilitating the flow of arms into Lebanon, the United States was already bombing the border between Syria and Iraq. Bashar al-Assad insisted, however, that Syria lacked the equipment or resources to lock down a border of 650 kilometers and that, on October 5, 2005, he actually invited a U.S. congressional delegation to Damascus for talks on patrolling the border. But that offer and others like it apparently went unanswered. Within two weeks, Husbaya, an Iraqi city on the border with Syria, had suffered the effects of a major offensive, and in other clashes with American troops on Syrian territory, a number of Syrians were killed.[13]

George W. Bush had already labeled Syria and Iran "allies of convenience" with Islamic terrorists. With the Israeli invasion of Gaza and Lebanon, however, the situation grew more serious. The United States chose to blame the new conflagration in the Middle East on Damascus and Tehran—both for supporting Hamas and Hezbollah and for not restraining them. The Israeli military offensive nearly provoked a reaction by Syria, and the United States would have liked nothing better. Perhaps Syria wanted to use Hezbollah as a surrogate or hoped to use the collapse of the central government in Lebanon as the basis for reestablishing its control over that country. But this remains a matter of speculation. It is clear that the unqualified support for Israel and the belligerent public statements of the

Bush administration have led to improved relations between Syria and Iran and hardened their support for their clients.[14] The situation is complicated. Syria did not support Saddam Hussein in the Iran-Iraq War, but President al-Assad must be experiencing some unease at the thought that Iran is now the dominant power in the region and that Iraq is no longer a countervailing force. He is undoubtedly aware that a "special mission unit" has been assigned to target foreign supporters of the Iraqi insurgency, and his concern over continuing American air strikes against Syria was palpable.[15] Given the explosive situation in Lebanon, and its devastated economy and infrastructure, it is also quite possible that what the president told us was true and that Syria really doesn't have a compelling interest in reestablishing control over Lebanon. Although President al-Assad has been aiding Hamas, moreover, it is not fully clear what enormous benefits might be gained from the rapidly deteriorating social conditions and the political chaos generated by the heightened rivalry for power between competing factions in Palestine. For all these reasons, without referencing his statements to our group, President al-Assad might be willing to entertain a serious diplomatic initiative. James Baker of the Iraq Study Group, who was also a former secretary of state, has called for just such an attempt by the United States.

Syrian receptivity to such an initiative would obviously depend upon a cessation of military activities on its border, a tempering of the overblown rhetoric by the Bush administration, and assurances that the United States is not intent on finding a pretext, such as the turbulence in Lebanon, the Hariri affair, or the Iraq debacle, to undertake yet another instance of regime change. Actions of this sort and diplomatic assurances, however, have not been forthcoming. President al-Assad told us that in a meeting with Colin Powell, for example, the secretary of state stated quite forthrightly that "peace is not a priority" in the relationship between the United States and Syria. President al-Assad noted with disgust that three U.S. congressional delegations were denied access to Syria by the State Department. According to him, American officials were also unwilling to meet with the new Syrian delegation to Iraq in Baghdad. Finally, in what he clearly perceived to be a personal as well as a political insult, he and his wife were denied visas to the United States, where he was scheduled to participate in meetings about the relationship between Lebanon and Syria and address the UN General Assembly.[16]

Blundering diplomacy of this sort has left the Bush administration without much credibility in Syria. As Lebanon was being blown to bits by Israel, the United States called on Egypt and Saudi Arabia to act as proxies to quell the crisis, drive a wedge between Syria and Iran, and pressure President al-Assad into abandoning his support for Hezbollah.[17] But there is little reason why the Syrians should adopt this course of action. The United States withdrew its ambassador to Syria in the aftermath of the Hariri crisis, direct talks have not occurred, economic sanctions remain in place, incentives have not been specified, and the Bush administration's public statements about Syria remain belligerent and uncompromising.

President al-Assad stated his willingness to press for a cease-fire in the context of a general peace initiative for the region that would include a swap of prisoners between Israel and Hezbollah and the return of the Golan Heights to Syria.[18] The president's position is consistent with his earlier proposal for a joint U.S.-Syria patrol of the border with Iraq, and he spoke with us of his 2003 proposal to the United Nations for a nuclear-free zone—including Israel—in the Middle East. He insisted that two peace initiatives regarding Israel had been forwarded to the United States, but he had received no response to either. The same fate awaited his initiatives for ending the

Lebanese invasion by Israel. No dialogue exists between Syria and the United States, no trust, and—without the participation of Syria—no possibility for sustained peace in the region.

President al-Assad spoke to us of the pressure applied by the U.S. State Department to prevent businesses from selling computer parts to Syria and the ongoing attempt to isolate Syria internationally and label it a rogue state. His minister of education, the former dean of the medical school and president of Damascus University, told us that he had tried to build relations with thirty different American universities while on a personal tour, but nothing came of his efforts. The president was clearly appalled by the attitudes of American policy makers to his overtures and, though it is difficult to take their rhetoric seriously, terribly concerned that the United States was intent on producing what neoconservatives have called a "creative chaos" out of which a new democracy might be hatched.

Bashar al-Assad had a hint of despair in his voice when he told us that although our two nations had had many disputes, for the first time, the peaceful intentions of the United States in the Middle East are not taken seriously by anyone. He seemed painfully aware that Syria is far weaker than Iran and that geopolitically—given its proximity to Lebanon, Iraq, and Pakistan—it is a tempting target for invasion. We could sense that he knew that his father's policies had isolated Syria even within the Arab community and that the region's stability was crumbling due to U.S. policies in Iraq and Israel's intransigence in dealing with Palestine. But there was also a note of defiance. President al-Assad stated that it was impossible to talk about stabilizing Lebanon or quelling the insurgency in Iraq without Syria's involvement. He warned that the Bush administration had not conquered the hearts and minds of the Arab citizens and that an attack on his regime would produce a national resistance on a par with that in Iraq. That was where we left things.

U.S. Academics for Peace took what we heard seriously. We all agreed that the president of Syria was not the naïve fool that the Western media had made him out to be. He also seemed to be a person with whom one might disagree, but with whom it was nonetheless possible to talk reasonably. It therefore seemed only sensible for our report to call on Secretary of State Condoleezza Rice to initiate a large-scale and serious dialogue with Syrian officials at all levels, with the intention of promoting peace and avoiding the language and actions of war. This meeting made it clear to us that dialogue was necessary to determine what was self-serving and what was not in President Bashar al-Assad's arguments. But even more ominously, it was clear that, without dialogue, only more violence, misunderstandings, and instability are likely for the region in the future.

6

Withdrawal Pains

Gaza, Lebanon, and the Future of Palestine

Before my first trip to the Occupied Territories in 2004 with a delegation organized by the Faculty for Israeli-Palestinian Peace, I was a rather conventional left-wing critic of Israeli policy. I knew that the condition of the Palestinian refugees was bad, but until I saw for myself what had transpired in towns such as Jenin and Jayousz, I had no idea just how bad. Of all the places I have visited, only there did I experience such shock and such a palpable feeling of oppression. Having grown up in the Washington Heights section of New York, a neighborhood of German-Jewish exiles where every second family had lost relatives in the Holocaust, I felt even more ashamed of Israeli policies—tantamount to ethnic cleansing—that remain acceptable largely because they remain unseen. I was even more shocked when I learned from any number of Israeli friends how few of their countrymen and -women, let alone Americans or American Jews, had actually visited the territories and the people living under the heel of their state.

Upon my return, I edited an issue of *Logos: A Journal of Modern Society and Culture* devoted to Palestine, and it sparked a radical growth in readership. Then, along with well-known literary critic Bruce Robbins and noted psychologist Jessica Benjamin, I helped organize a conference on the plight of the Palestinians that drew about five hundred people at Columbia University. It was immediately criticized for its lack of balance—Palestine was the focus, rather than Israel or Israel and Palestine—as if Fox News or CNN or even the *New York Times* is known for its balanced presentation of the Palestinian point of view. Things have changed somewhat since then, but the United States remains a staunch supporter of Israel,[1] and the satisfaction of Israeli interests is still seen by the United States as a precondition for the satisfaction of all other interests in the region.[2] Emotional loyalties make it difficult to engage in any critical discussion of Israeli policy, and the problem has only grown since the Israeli disengagement from Gaza.

Here I would like to evaluate that policy and what has transpired in its wake. The removal of eight thousand Jewish settlers from Gaza in 2005 was a daring tactic. It was originally conceived as the initial phase of a broader withdrawal from the West Bank that would allow Israel to set its borders unilaterally without engaging the Palestinians in negotiations. The result would be a set of isolated cantons constructed around large Jewish settlements and isolated by a "wall of separation," which would leave the new state of Palestine without a contiguous territory.[3] The possibility existed of linking this withdrawal to new negotiations and an Israeli retreat to the boundaries in existence before the 1967 war. But this possibility was effectively nullified by the electoral victory of Hamas in January 2006, which was partially due to the lack of progress in peace negotiations and this organization's stubborn refusal to either recognize Israel or disavow armed struggle.

Initially, with the help of the United States, Israel sought to destabilize the new government by economic means.[4] When that proved unsuccessful, however, more brutal methods came into play. Sparked by the capture of an Israeli solider by the small terrorist group known as Islamic Jihad and then by the capture of two more Israeli soldiers by the Lebanese branch of Hezbollah[5]—actions apparently predicated on the belief that these soldiers could be exchanged for Palestinian prisoners languishing in Israeli jails and a trio of Lebanese hostages taken in 2004[6]—Israel sought to destroy its most dangerous foe.[7] It began a two-front assault on Gaza and Lebanon that resulted in hundreds of civilian deaths and billions of dollars in damage to property and infrastructure in Lebanon, as well as demolition of the lone power station and many of the ports, roads, and government buildings in Gaza. The Israeli nation, so lauded for its democratic character, once again engaged in a policy of collective punishment that ultimately proved self-defeating. It undermined the tepid support by states attempting to moderate more intemperate tendencies in the Middle East, such as Egypt; fostered an increase of anti-Semitism; and radically subverted support for Israel in the world community. The frustration produced by Israel's incursion into Lebanon and Palestine would only become magnified, given the initial hope engendered by the withdrawal from Gaza.

Was it a breakthrough or a ploy? Since the plan to withdraw between eight thousand and nine thousand Jewish settlers from Gaza in mid-August 2005 was first announced by Prime Minister Ariel Sharon, its character and its meaning have been hotly debated by those concerned with the future of the Occupied Territories and the possibilities for peace. The Bush administration and the *New York Times* greeted the Israeli plan with great enthusiasm. In contrast, many critics, whose primary concern was the plight of the Palestinians, insisted that the withdrawal should not be supported because Sharon was an inveterate liar and, more important, because it was necessary—as Uri Avinery put it—to think about "the day after."[8]

Whether Sharon was a liar or not, he bet his legacy on this

undertaking. Sharon took risks in implementing his new policy. It resulted in various no-confidence votes, threatened to split his Likud Party, and created the distinct possibility of civil strife among Israelis. It easily could have resulted in his fall from power. Large right-wing demonstrations of "orange shirts" took place, and the most fanatical among the settlers correctly understood the withdrawal from Gaza as a precedent that might shatter their dream of a "Greater Israel." Popular sympathy was extended to the zealots by an Israeli media increasingly obsessed with the self-pitying diaries of teenage imperialists and the pseudophilosophy of half-addled right-wing rabbis.[9] Sharon's commitment to his new initiative thus had to be taken seriously. Simply opposing the withdrawal would have provided objective support for those who believe that any "concession" is tantamount to an appeasement of terrorism. Or, to put it another way, on the "day after" the initiative was rejected, the ultraimperialists and the religious fanatics would have been much stronger than they were before.

Although skepticism is appropriate when thinking about the original withdrawal from Gaza, it must be married with the recognition that, though not a giant step toward peace, the initiative offered new possibilities for resolving the ongoing conflict between the Israelis and the Palestinians. These possibilities have been put on hold by the Israelis' reentry into Gaza and their invasion of Lebanon. But the idea that the United States (or neoconservatives in the United States) somehow forced Sharon's hand—an argument made after the fact, mostly by ultraleftists who doubted the sincerity of his plan—is patently absurd.[10] Besides there being a lack of evidence, the political risks taken by Sharon were simply incommensurate with whatever financial or political pressure the United States might have brought to bear. Withdrawing from Gaza along with four towns on the West Bank—Jericho, Jayousz, Qualquilya, and Tulkarm—was a bold proposal that created hysteria among religious fundamentalists and Zionist extremists. That the Israeli government chose to react as it did to the provocations of Hezbollah and the Islamic Jihad in 2006 does not change that reality. The military actions undertaken by Israel against Lebanon and the Palestinians proved to be a victory for the same nationalist, xenophobic, and ultrareligious forces whose rhetoric inspired the assassination of Prime Minister Yitzhak Rabin and who maintain the vision of a "Greater Israel" that extends from Jordan to the Mediterranean.

In a way, the withdrawal also reflected a coming to terms with what seemed to be a growing malaise within Israel. Deepening moral uncertainty and a lack of belief in its own ideals have become increasingly palpable over the last few years in Israel. With respect to much of the world community, the country is on the verge of becoming a pariah nation. Just as the invasion of Lebanon and the reentry into Gaza were one provincial way to deal with these problems, the withdrawal was another. The new policy not only confronted the increasing identification of Sharon's Likud Party with an intractable fanaticism in the public eye but also implicitly contested the way that a cluster of tiny settlements—like the few hundred Jewish settlers situated among tens of thousands of Arabs in Hebron—had been holding Israeli policy hostage.[11] Their continued defense had cost the state a fortune and created risks of violence that were incommensurate with the potential benefits.

Gaza was an economically unsustainable wasteland even before the new Israeli incursion of 2006. It may have a fine beach on its border "strip," which served as the home for most of its Jewish settlers, but human rights groups such as B'Tselem and the Mezan Center for Human Rights in Gaza estimated that at the start of 2005 more than 28,000 people in the Gaza Strip were rendered homeless and an equal number required home repairs as a result of Israeli military incursions. Unemployment stood at more than 65 percent, and the poverty rate was more than 75 percent. In spite of the fact that the West Bank has almost double the population, half of all Palestinian deaths since September 2000 have occurred in Gaza.[12] The four West Bank towns in question, all staunchly opposed to the Israeli occupation, were never economically important. All were essentially ungovernable by Israel and, except for Jericho, blocked off by the wall of separation. The wall's extension under cover of the withdrawal will now divide even more neighborhoods and cut off more than 55,000 Palestinians living in East Jerusalem by placing them outside the barrier. As for the Jewish settlers in Gaza who needed to be relocated, they constituted a tiny fraction of the 250,000 remaining in the West Bank, not to mention the other 200,000 in East Jerusalem.[13] The withdrawal distracted the Western press from the more than 11,000 housing units being built in the Occupied Territories and the 3,500 between East Jerusalem and the 30,000-person community of Maale Adumim, which will create a contiguous Jewish area and basically divide the West Bank.

President George W. Bush and Secretary of State Condoleezza Rice called for a "full stop" to the construction of new settlements, noting that such activity threatens the "road map" to peace. But Sharon remained firm when he met with the president at his ranch in Crawford, Texas, in April 2005. He made it clear that Jerusalem and Maale Adumim would be linked, "major Israeli population centers" in the West Bank would be "thickened," the "wall" would curl around the larger settlements, and none of them would be removed under any final status agreement. The "right of return" by Palestinians was denied outright, and Sharon insisted that the "new realities" made it "unrealistic" to expect a return to the pre-1967 borders, or what is known as the "green line." Such comments did not interfere with Bush's praise for this "strong visionary leader" and his "courageous initiative" to withdraw from Gaza. The old fox even got the United States to offer an unspecified package for economic development of the Negev and Galilee for resettling the settlers.[14] It was a bravura performance by Sharon.

Too little attention was paid, especially outside of Israel, to how the withdrawal from Gaza was used as a justification for expanding the Jewish settlements on the West Bank. About seventy thousand Israeli settlers might well remain beyond the wall and exist as an obviously irredentist minority entrenched in any future Palestinian state. Most Palestinians will likely live outside the confines of the wall, even though it will surround fifty-three Palestinian communities on at least three sides. Forgotten are those who will lose farmland and access to roads and other towns. The wall of separation will ensure the protection of lands that have already been taken by settlers, as well as fragmentation of the colonized. The withdrawal also created a situation in which unilateral decision making has replaced negotiation with respect to the geography of borders, the roads connecting Jewish settlements, the working of checkpoints, and the degree of practical sovereignty of a Palestinian state.[15]

The withdrawal left the inhabitants of Gaza in something akin to an outdoor prison. Israel actually ceded nothing: it retained control of airspace, roads, and the right to intervene—whenever it wished—in what would remain a "demilitarized" area. Even the decision on whether to build an airport or a seaport in Gaza ultimately rested with Israel. It all sounded good, but this demilitarized territory left the Palestinian Authority in difficult straits when it came to dealing with the organized resistance groups (often armed with better weapons than the official police) that have thrived since the beginning of the Second Intifada. Should negotiations between the Israelis and the Palestinians ever resume, moreover, the framework for any treaty will be a state carved around areas that the Israelis do not want and in which the Palestinians cannot prosper.

Other ways of thinking about the withdrawal make one's skin crawl. Gaza could, conceivably, be turned into some kind of buffer zone between Israelis and Palestinians.[16] Some suggested—prophetically—that the withdrawal would be used as a cover for remilitarizing the entire area and engaging in a direct assault on the population.[17] That took place in November 2006 when Israel entered Gaza once again and shelled it mercilessly, leading to the deaths of eighteen members of a single family in Beit Hanoun. Other dire possibilities are not of a military nature. There has been much talk concerning what Benjamin Netanyahu termed the "demographic threat" to the Jewish identity of the state posed by Israeli Arabs, whose birthrate is three times that of Israeli Jews. Should a sovereign Palestinian state not emerge on the border of Israel, and should domestic conflict between Arabs and Jews intensify in Israel, Gaza might serve as the perfect dumping ground for a population transfer. This possibility is, perhaps, remote. In the Middle East, however, it is always important to retain a sense of the worst. The most dangerous implications of the withdrawal need to be articulated not merely for the sake of Palestinians but for Israeli Arabs as well.

The withdrawal still generates a glint of optimism following the Israeli military action of 2006. It whets the demand for further withdrawals, with an eye on the creation of a viable Palestinian state. If publicly interpreted in this way, Israel's unilateral withdrawal from Gaza can be linked to the need to restart bilateral negotiations. Unless linkages of this sort are made, however, new initiatives can have little positive impact. The withdrawal from Gaza retains meaning only if it becomes part of a larger enterprise concerned with creating the foundations of a viable Palestinian state. The last formula provided at Camp David in 2000, beyond quibbling over what percentage of land was actually being returned, offered the Palestinians a set of disconnected bantustans that would have made sovereignty untenable. It is not likely that the offer will improve in the aftermath of the recent military campaign, let alone the new linkage between East Jerusalem and Maale Adumim and the use of the wall to isolate Kalandia, Akkab, Anata, and the Shufat refugee camp from other Arab neighborhoods. If the past is any indication, Israel's next proposal with respect to the actual size of Palestine will be less than what it offered in 2000.[18] The real question is whether a smaller and even less tenable state will prove acceptable to the Palestinians and what reaction the rejection of such an offer might produce.

Unfortunately, the frenzy created by the withdrawal from Gaza is precisely what has caused that question to be ignored. The Middle East has often suffered from what Tocqueville originally termed a "crisis of rising expectations." The withdrawal from Gaza generated new longings and expectations that, if the past is again any indication, will result in violence should they be unfulfilled. Thousands of Palestinian towns have already been destroyed, the economy of the Occupied Territories is in shambles, the humiliating crossings and checkpoints remain, and the arrests and extrajudicial executions continue. The wall, the settlements, compensation for the right of return, and ultimately the borders and integrity of Palestine—and the roughly $2.5 billion per year in aid plus the $2.5 billion in loans to Israel by the United States—must remain in the forefront of efforts to liberate the Occupied Territories. The situation has only gotten worse since the military incursion into Gaza and the invasion of Lebanon in 2006.

Those concerned with justice in the Middle East have no option but to integrate the prospect of a future withdrawal into their formulation of a more general strategy. They must reject either unbridled optimism or unqualified despair and think clearly about the ultimate question of a contiguous Palestinian state. It is, ironically, Israel that will experience the bolder implications of withdrawal. The temptation is overwhelming to latch on to this "solution" when more than 60 percent of Israelis desires a two-state solution. But for the Palestinians, if it must be construed as more than a ploy, it remains far less than a breakthrough. The task of their representatives remains one of creating linkages between the withdrawal from Gaza and a meaningful solution to the conflict. That is the case in spite of ongoing Israeli intransigence. Dogmatic opposition is, again, as misguided as unwarranted celebration. The extent to which the Palestinians and their progressive allies can navigate a course between these two poles is the extent to which—ultimately—the withdrawal can serve as a step along the road to peace and the self-determination of a people.

As of 2007, Israel has existed more than twice as long *with* control over Palestinian territories as without. The occupation of Palestine can no longer be considered merely temporary. The argument that the costs of the occupation are too high is belied by an extraordinary Israeli economic growth rate of 6.6 percent in 2005, and the quality of the deals offered to the Palestinians by Israel has deteriorated since 1948. The lack of tangible progress toward creating a Palestinian state helped bring about the electoral triumph of Hamas: 78 percent of the Palestinian citizenry voted, and Hamas received 75 of 132 parliamentary seats. Palestinians expressed their contempt for the corruption and bureaucratic ineptness of Fatah, and they blamed the organization created by Yasir Arafat in 1980 for its inability to deliver the goods and its failure to stand up to the Israeli oppressor. Israel evidenced little sense of the way Hamas had ingratiated itself through efficient social programs and the moral imprimatur of religious conviction.[19] The degree of support accorded Hamas by the Palestinians may finally explain why Arafat and his successor, Mahmoud Abbas, were unable to "disarm the terrorists," as the Americans and Israelis insisted they should. In any event, the victory of Hamas has given Israel several possible options: it can fix its borders through further unilateral withdrawals from the West Bank; formally annex previously held territories; attempt to destabilize the new regime, possibly through military action; or negotiate with a Palestinian government in which Hamas plays an important role.

Even before military action was undertaken in Gaza, the stunning and unanticipated electoral victory of Hamas had already minimized any Israeli interest in eliminating the wall, sharing Jerusalem, negotiating the right of return, stopping the construction of new settlements, or dealing with those that had already been constructed. There is now a general consensus on keeping Jerusalem, defending the three major blocks of settlements, continuing to build new settlements, attempting to annex 58 percent of the West Bank (including "security zones"), and manipulating violence or the threat of violence by extremist elements in the Palestinian community. It is hard to imagine a deal predicated on these conditions that would allow for an economically viable Palestine. As compensation, following the military assault of 2006, Prime Minister Ehud Olmert indicated his willingness to engage in new unilateral withdrawals from poverty-stricken towns—or towns that Israel could not control anyway—with relatively small numbers of settlers. Handing them over in lieu of creating a viable Palestinian state would surely prove financially and militarily prudent. Such gestures probably would also create a flood of positive publicity. From the standpoint of the Israeli leadership, if a Palestinian government were able to deal with these new acquisitions, so much the better; if not, then, as with Gaza, Israel could always exercise the option of reentering those relinquished cities and restoring order or perhaps even reclaiming them.

From the beginning, Olmert refused to negotiate with Hamas or with any government in which it played a significant role as a coalition partner, and he openly stated his desire to destabilize the new regime. Olmert began by holding talks with President Abbas, to the chagrin of Hamas. He then moved to constrain travel by Palestinians and withhold customs payments by Israel amounting to more than $55 million per month, and he called on the United States to do the same with regard to $300 million in humanitarian aid.[20] Olmert raised the ante, however, after primitive rockets from Gaza shelled the town of Ashkelon and two soldiers were killed and a nineteen-year-old corporal named Gilad Shalit was captured by members of Islamic Jihad. It did not matter that thirty Palestinians, including three children and a pregnant woman, had been killed in the preceding weeks. Unconcerned with a response in proportion to what Israel had suffered, oblivious of any understanding of "reasonable culpability," Olmert unleashed a brutal two-pronged assault on both the north and south of Gaza. Dozens of Palestinians were killed and hundreds more wounded. The only power generator in Gaza was destroyed, leaving 1.5 million people and its two main hospitals without electricity or water in a region where summer temperatures reach 120 degrees. Also destroyed were various bridges, roads, schools, and buildings housing the Ministry of the Interior, the president, and the headquarters of Fatah.[21]

The kidnapping of two Israeli soldiers by Hezbollah followed, and Israel reacted with an invasion prepared by a campaign of merciless bombing. More than eleven hundred were killed, tens of thousands wounded, and nearly a million displaced; damage to property and infrastructure reached $4 billion. But things did not go as anticipated. One hundred Israeli citizens were also killed, houses were destroyed, and everyday life was disrupted by the rocket attacks of Hezbollah. The aura of invincibility surrounding the Israeli army was pierced as Israel became bogged down in the conflict. Moreover, as parts of Lebanon were being systematically obliterated, Hezbollah and Hamas were gaining new sympathy throughout the Arab world. It did not seem to matter that the lives and well-being of Lebanese and Palestinian civilians were being sacrificed less for concrete ends than for symbolic ones. The brutal policy undertaken by Israel has been completely counterproductive. As it won what Gramsci termed the war of position in the present, Israel has begun losing the war of maneuver that looms in the future. The invasion was devoid of aims commensurate with the losses that the Arab side in particular has suffered. War aims involved little more than Israel seeking to destroy its "terrorist enemies" and creating a buffer zone on the Lebanese border, and Hezbollah jockeying for position in Lebanon and leadership in the Arab struggle against the "Zionist entity."

When the UN Security Council finally overcame the strategy of delay employed by the Unites States so that Israel would have time to further its military goals, the measure it passed on August 12 did not touch on the exchange of prisoners that had sparked the conflict in the first place or the question of the Golan Heights or even a fixed border between Israel and Lebanon. The motion of the Security Council—mindful of the United States' unqualified support of Israel—did not deal with the matter of disarming Hezbollah or the possibility of future "defensive" incursions by Israel into Lebanon. Although it banned arms sales to the Lebanese government, a clause obviously directed against Iran and Syria, it did not ban arms sales to Israel by the United States. Nor did the United Nations insist that Israel withdraw from the fertile Sheeba Farms area, and nothing was said about Gaza or the Palestinians. Israel was called on to pull back its forces, and a buffer between Israel and Lebanon was set up, presumably so that major Israeli cities would no longer be in range of Hezbollah rockets. Thirty thousand troops were introduced (half from the United Nations and half from Lebanon) to patrol this no-man's-land—thereby saving Israel the trouble—thus ending the fighting between the two nations.[22] Nevertheless, the imbalance of power between Israel and its neighbors—especially Palestine—will continue, along with the absence of an enduring peace.

Still, it should be noted that no matter how lopsided the balance of power between Israel and Palestine, an event like the invasion of Gaza is not constituted by only one side.[23] To somehow bracket the Palestinians (or their political representatives) from the conditions that produced an event of this magnitude is to deprive them and those acting in their name of agency and freedom. The brutal and inhuman "retaliatory" assault that resulted in such destruction should have been expected: Israel has done the same thing often enough.[24] It was a terrible decision by Islamic Jihad to abduct that soldier in the first place. Just as bad was the decision by Hamas to call for "conditional negotiations" with Israel about his release—the condition being the freeing of all Palestinian women and more than thirty men currently in Israeli jails before negotiations could begin. The combination of capturing the soldier and then offering negotiating terms that Israel would never accept created the pretext for its military offensive against Gaza.

The stubborn refusal of Hamas to recognize the existence of the fourth strongest military power in the world obviously did not help matters, and it allowed Israel, once again, to claim the lack of a "negotiating partner." As for Fatah, following the elections that brought Hamas to power, its activists demonstrated in the streets of Gaza, shot their guns into the air, and burned abandoned cars outside the parliament building as they demanded the resignation of corrupt party officials and insisted that no coalition be formed between the two main political organizations of Palestine. The future threatens to be a repeat of the past: Hamas has stated its willingness to suspend the "truce" with Israel and, once again, employ suicide bombers; Fatah is in a state of paralysis; and military organizations such as Islamic Jihad and the Al Akysa brigade, acting without any hint of democratic accountability to the Palestinian citizenry, continue to exert a veto over any possibility of pursuing negotiations for peace through their practice of terrorist violence. The erosion of hope is occurring on both sides of the wall.

Of course, the point is not to blame the victim. Rather, it is to insist that the victim here is not the political elite but the citizenry of Palestine. There is a tendency to equate the two, but that is a mistake. Infighting between Palestinian organizations has decentralized power to the point where civil war looms amid the devastation wrought by an enemy with a vastly superior military arsenal. And in spite of the nonsense spread by the media, no one has appeared as a genuine successor to Arafat. Palestinian politicians and organizations are clearly operating in extraordinarily difficult and constrained conditions. But they must bear some responsibility for policies that waver between revenge and surrender. The political establishment has been blind to the political implications deriving from the existing imbalance of military power, unwilling to tailor their demands to accept the reality that the Palestinians will be the weaker partner in any negotiation, and cynical in their readiness to sacrifice the people for their own ambitions.

There is nothing abstract about discussing these problems, even amid the ruins of Gaza and Lebanon. Israel will ultimately withdraw once again, and new conditions for diplomatic action and national decision making will emerge. No matter what organization, or coalition of organizations, represents the Palestinians in the future, it will have to confront the challenge of ruling without a viable contiguous state. With an enemy like Israel, which has little incentive to negotiate and every incentive to disrupt the creation of a stable government, this will be no easy task. But that does not change the reality. Gaza was descending into bureaucratic anarchy, poverty, and lawlessness following the Israeli withdrawal and before the latest military action took place. Elections do not guarantee sovereignty or stability. Providing the Palestinian state with a monopoly over the means of coercion and establishing a centralized bureaucracy are the preconditions for bringing about meaningful progress for the Palestinian people. The tactics for achieving this aim must be determined by the leadership of the different factions within Palestine, but the strategic imperative should be clear to anyone. It involves disarming the gangs and private militias, centralizing the bureaucracy, and creating a broader and more accountable understanding of the national interest.

As the social and political situation in Gaza continues to deteriorate, and as civil war looms between competing factions, the future looks increasingly bleak for the Palestinians. Among the most interesting positive signs, perhaps, is the "Prisoners Manifesto." Composed by Murwan Barghouti and other Palestinian activists jailed in Israel on charges of terrorism (the irony here is unmistakable), it offers the basis for an agreement between Fatah, Hamas, and the various smaller military organizations currently at odds with one another. That document, which essentially serves as the basis for a national unity government, calls on Israel to accept the borders existing prior to the 1967 war as the basis for a Palestinian state, recognize the right of return, and partition Jerusalem.[25] Some suggest that the new prospect for unity provided by this manifesto actually spurred the Israeli military action against Gaza. More to the point, it is difficult to imagine what would lead Israel to accept its terms. Still, the complex negotiations among the prisoners, who are all important representatives of different Palestinian factions, could not have occurred without the tacit permission of Israeli authorities. With the military offensive against Gaza, the retaking of its northern region, and the likelihood of future incursions by Israel, the possibility of bringing a Palestinian state into existence seems more remote than ever. Nevertheless, with an eye lingering on Gaza, the struggle continues, and there remains what Manes Sperber called "the bitter taste of hope."

7

The Middle East Spills Over

The Sudan and the Crisis in Darfur

The Middle East is not merely a geographical designation but a cauldron of ideological and material conflicts. Its borders are arbitrary. Neither religious intolerance nor ancient tribal and ethnic hatreds respect them. Conflicts of this sort have been rife in the Sudan. It is a huge country roughly the size of western Europe, the largest in Africa, and it borders nine other states. The Islamic-Arab world intersects with Africa in the Sudan. Its oil- and resource-rich provinces in the south, most of whose citizens embrace Christianity or animism,[1] have for decades been resisting the authoritarian government of the north, with its strong Muslim mass base. Overlapping with these traditional religious tensions are roving groups of armed bandits, blood feuds, tribal hatreds, conflicts between cattle herders and farmers, and an ongoing competition over shrinking natural resources, livestock, and water. Such is the landscape for the civil conflict that has been taking place off and on since the early 1950s, which has decimated the Sudan as surely as the Hundred Years War once destroyed Europe.

Darfur, which constitutes the western part of the Sudan, is administratively divided into three parts running from north to south. Darfur is nearly the size of France and is marked by 153 squalid camps for millions of internally displaced persons (IDPs). These refugees fled their villages to escape the Sudanese military and the armed bandits on horseback known as the Janjaweed. Such roving marauders were organized by the government of President Omar Hassan Al-Bashir in Khartoum to quell the ongoing rebellion in the region. Hunger, thirst, disease, filth, the threat of rape and other violence, and a stultifying idleness abound in these IDP camps, with their sea of thatched huts, flimsy tents, and mud streets. The refugees wish only to return to their villages. But repatriating them, rebuilding their homes, and compensating the victims for what they have undergone is an expensive undertaking. Issues of this sort, coupled with the government's unwillingness to disarm the Janjaweed, are at the root of the controversy concerning implementation of the Comprehensive Peace Agreement of January 2006 and the Darfur Peace Agreement of May 2006, brokered by the African Union.[2]

A new bombing campaign by the Khartoum government against Darfur in August and September 2006 drove tens of thousands more villagers into the camps, and the ten thousand troops amassed by the Al-Bashir regime might drive the IDPs over the border or disband the camps entirely, leading to death on a massive scale. About seven thousand troops from the African Union were stationed in Darfur to protect the camps, but they have been harshly criticized for their incompetence and inexperience. Even before September 30, 2006, when the mandate of the African Union troops was set to expire, the requisite funds for maintaining them had almost run out. On August 31, the UN Security Council passed a resolution calling for "rehatting" some of them, adding a few thousand civilian police, and mixing them with roughly seventeen thousand UN troops. This force would be used to protect the refugees from the Janjaweed and the Sudanese military in the future. Nevertheless, President Al-Bashir was adamant in his refusal to either extend the mandate of the troops from the African Union or allow the United Nations to intervene in Sudanese affairs.

Many refugees living in the IDP camps would undoubtedly welcome UN intervention. This is also true of certain rebel groups such as the Justice and Equality Movement led by Khalil Ibrahim and the Sudanese Liberation Movement army faction led by Abdelwahid Mohamed al-Nur, which have refused to sign the Darfur Peace Agreement, thereby initiating conflicts with other oppositional groups that have signed and heightening instability in the region.[3] Some have even insisted that it would be best for all concerned if the southern region of the Sudan and Darfur were to secede. Given the wealth of oil and other resources in the south and its natural concern with national sovereignty, however, the Khartoum government will do everything possible to prevent that from happening. In Khartoum no less than in Iran, Libya, and elsewhere, anti-Western radicals have argued that the United Nations is nothing more than a front for "imperialist powers" intent on "recolonizing" the Sudan. As anti-Western rhetoric increased, the bad press suffered by the Sudan was routinely attributed to Jewish control over the media. Such charges were mostly self-serving propaganda. But the toppling of the Taliban in Afghanistan, the American occupation of Iraq, and the generally uncritical support extended by the United States to Israel lent credence to such charges in some quarters.[4]

Censorship and the assault on civil liberties were less stringent in the six months after the signing of the Comprehensive Peace Agreement. However, with the perception of a rising threat from abroad, domestic repression by the Al-Bashir regime intensified. Governmental surveillance tightened, newspapers were shut down, and street demonstrations were disbanded by the police. But as far as any "regime change" is concerned, its beneficiaries would most likely not be the "democratic parties" run by families and grounded in tribal loyalties but rather the Islamic fundamentalists, who—in spite of the split between moderate and extremist elements—constitute the only genuinely mass movement in the Sudan.[5]

The impact of an invasion by UN troops on a singularly multicultural nation the size of the Sudan is impossible to predict. But it is possible to imagine that a national resistance will take shape and that IDPs living in the camps might find themselves caught in a maelstrom far worse than that which has gripped Iraq. Eighty tribes in the Sudan have their own militias, previous peace agreements are in doubt, Islamic fundamentalists are training in the Jebel Marra Mountains, and the country seems set to implode.

Such were my thoughts as I deplaned in Khartoum on September 3, 2006, along with thirteen other academics (mostly Americans) representing Conscience International. We were there to participate in a two-day conference that would be attended by a host of leading Sudanese politicians and academics. The humanitarian activist and leader of our delegation, Dr. Jim Jennings, had performed a herculean task in securing our visas and, in cooperation with our hosts, organizing what would become a remarkably candid exchange of views. We took an excursion to the pyramids of the long vanished Kush civilization, visited the pharmaceutical factory mistakenly bombed under the orders of President Bill Clinton, and witnessed an extraordinary Sufi religious ritual; in addition, a visit to the Darfurian IDP camp of Abu Shouck, near El Fasher, was organized at the last minute. Our group was treated with great respect and hospitality by the Council for International People's Friendship and its influential secretary-general, Ahmed Abd Al-Rahman Mohammed, and Hasim El-Tinay of the Institute for Internal Peace and Dialogue.

An atmosphere of crisis hung over Khartoum. We quickly learned about the Sudanese dislike for the condescension and provincialism exhibited by American diplomats—something I had heard everywhere in my travels through the Middle East—and we noted the chilly interaction between these politicians and diplomats from two very different worlds. Because we were not professional politicians or diplomatic representatives of the United States, but cosmopolitan academics engaged in citizen diplomacy, we were able to engage the Sudanese in a frank manner. As for the conference, which was videotaped, various panels dealt with possible ways to restructure the Sudanese educational system and the opportunities for investment. My panel, which dealt explicitly with the crisis in Darfur, was chaired by the former Sudanese ambassador to the United States, Charles Manyang. On my left, in a smart business suit, was the governmental minister Dr. El-Tijani Mustafa, who defended official policies and denied the organized employment of the Janjaweed in Darfur; on my right, dressed in beautiful white robes and a white turban, was Dr. Abdelrahman Dosa, who subjected official policy to a sober critique. He explained how the Janjaweed were being used by Khartoum both for murderous purposes and to pursue a civil war on the cheap against citizens and rebels in Darfur as well as in southern Sudan.

My presentation on September 6 explored ways to defuse the international crisis and overcome the apparent hardening of positions in both the Sudan and the West. I was struck by how seriously the audience took what I said, and I soon learned the reason why. For all the public rhetoric, Khartoum was looking for an exit—"with honor"—from the crisis its leaders had so unconscionably created. I made a number of suggestions in my talk, the most important of which concerned the need to rethink the question of military deployment by the United Nations. Dr. Nasir Elseed of the Islamic Socialist Party and Aldondoni Deng of the National Congress Party greeted it with enthusiasm. Sheik Ahmed Abd Al-Rahman told me on

September 7 that he would deliver my working paper, along with his own comments, to the two Sudanese vice presidents and that it would be "discussed further."

The first indication that Khartoum was becoming more flexible on extending the mandate of the African Union troops was made public on September 11, 2006, and adding four thousand troops was deemed acceptable. The mandate of these troops was then extended to December 30, 2006, with the possibility of a further extension to April 1, 2007. On September 14, in Addis Ababa, the Sudanese state minister for foreign affairs, Al-Samani Al-Wasila, called for a "partnership" among the African Union, the Sudan, and the international community rather than enforced resolutions.[6] The *New York Times* subsequently reported on September 21, 2006, that the Sudanese government would allow "logistical" support from the United Nations to help the African Union. As funding was acquired from the Arab League and the European Union, willingness to accept logistical support turned into willingness to accept "military advisers" from the United Nations.[7] On October 6 a spokesman for UN Secretary-General Kofi Annan stated that he had received a letter from President Al-Bashir formally accepting the proposal concerning UN military support to the African Union mission in the Sudan. Finally, as reported on October 25, 2006, by the *South Africa News*, President Al-Bashir stated, "We have no objection to the African Union increasing its troops, strengthening its mandate, or even receiving logistical support from the European Union, the United Nations, or the Arab League for that matter, but this must, of course, be done in consultation with the government of national unity."

With revisions, and naturally without attribution, this position taken by the president reflected the most important recommendation made in my presentation. Maybe it was a coincidence, since there are often many voices urging the same policy. As the proverb says: success has many fathers; failure is an orphan. Conscience International was, however, clearly in the right place at the right time, and it seems that citizen diplomacy driven by goodwill always offers the prospect of a better outcome than does imperial hubris. In any event, the new position regarding a partnership was a prudent move by a Sudanese regime known for its stubbornness. But the new course is not set in stone, and there is no guarantee that it will be implemented. Further progress will depend on whether the United Nations, the United States, and Western opinion makers make the commitment not to act hastily but to engage with the Sudan—peacefully and patiently—in an attempt to resolve one of the most terrible crises of our time.

Positions had seemingly grown intractable when our conference began. It was as if—on a number of crucial issues—international organizations intent on preventing mass murder were facing off against an intractable authoritarian government concerned with preserving the sovereignty of the Sudan. If supporters of UN intervention seemed blind to constraints, the political issue with respect to dealing with the Sudanese was not whether their suspicions regarding the imperialist ambitions of the United Nations were legitimate but whether they *believed* them to be legitimate. Because it has often been a tool of Western great-power interests, and also because the United States has vetoed so many resolutions on behalf of Israel, the political intentions of the United Nations are still generally greeted with suspicion in much of the previously colonized world.

Suspicions of this sort made it important to emphasize that the United Nations is not identifiable merely with its Security Council, which is undemocratically constituted and weighted in favor of the more powerful Western states, or its General

Assembly, which is powerless other than with respect to articulating world opinion on any given matter. The United Nations also oversees the World Health Organization and UNESCO, along with various disaster relief agencies that have provided enormous help to the most unfortunate peoples, including the Palestinians. The UN Charter also recognizes the sovereignty of its member states and explicitly endorses the notion of national self-determination. Especially over the last few years, given its opposition to the American invasion of Iraq and the Israeli war on Lebanon, it is difficult to argue that the United Nations is simply a stand-in for the United States or that it is driven principally by imperialist designs on the Sudan.

Nevertheless, more sensitivity is necessary when dealing with the lingering memories of imperialism with regard to Africa in general and the Sudan in particular. That the Sudanese political leaders preoccupied themselves with defending the sovereignty of their country is only natural. Having said that, however, something else follows. Insofar as national self-determination is a universal right, those who lay claim to it must recognize that they are part of the international community. Thus, it would prove both unethical and impractical for the Sudan to simply turn inward.

An alternative was required—some middle ground between deploying either UN or Sudanese troops in Darfur. In philosophical terms, this called for mediating between abstract universal and provincial national concerns. Or, to put it another way, not two but three interests needed to be acknowledged. There was the interest in the human rights of southern dissidents and especially the IDPs in Darfur, which was the express concern of the United Nations and various disaster relief agencies; the interest of the Sudanese government in Khartoum; and, just as importantly, the regional interest represented by the African Union. Each of these interests, in my view, needed to be taken into account in sketching new ways of dealing with the issues pertinent to preventing further bloodshed in the Sudan. My aim, therefore, was not to resolve the conflict or provide definitive solutions to the problems facing the Sudan, Darfur, and the region. It was instead to offer a set of talking points that might provoke the formulation of more flexible policies, buy some time so that tempers might cool, and bring the opposing parties closer together. My arguments and proposals concerning the deployment of troops, the discovery of information, the activities of relief agencies, war crimes, and the sale of arms can be summarized as follows.

First, the United Nations was seeking to integrate, or "rehat," seventy-seven hundred African Union forces into a UN force of twenty-two thousand that would guarantee the safety of those living in the IDP camps dotting the landscape of Darfur. The Sudanese government adamantly rejected that idea and, instead, wished to employ ten thousand of its own troops to provide security. My suggestion for moving beyond the impasse called for extending the mandate and increasing the authority of the African Union. It proposed a change of focus that would rest on integrating Sudanese police or militia with military personnel from the United Nations and rehatting them under the command structure of the African Union. A check would thereby be provided on any "imperialist" designs by the United Nations, as well as on the more ominous ambitions of the regime in Khartoum, while privileging the potentially wide-ranging regional impact of the crisis. Such a plan would balance the Sudanese concern with national sovereignty, the needs of IDPs, and the broader interests of the region. It was never meant to offer any guarantee of success or any certainty that the ongoing humanitarian disaster would be brought to an end. It merely provided what, in my opinion, amounted to the best bet and an African solution to an African problem—the importance of which should not be underestimated.

Second, not only the United Nations but also various relief agencies fear that genocide is taking place in Darfur—although only the United States has officially used the term "genocide" in the present context. These organizations believe that 400,000 to 500,000 people have perished in the recent conflicts, while official Sudanese studies estimate the death toll at somewhere between 60,000 and 160,000. There is something profoundly disgusting about using numbers in this manner. But whose figures are correct is a matter of some importance. There is only one way of arriving at an answer: continue to allow independent investigators, who are guaranteed security by the Sudanese government, into Darfur. In fact, I suggested expanding the number of researchers and perhaps creating a set of international teams independent of any organization or state with a direct stake in the crisis. The more studies that emerge, the greater the likelihood of finding some consensual answers to pressing questions concerning the magnitude of events in Darfur, as well as their impact on nations such as Kenya, Ethiopia, Uganda, and the Central African Republic, which harbor more than 350,000 Sudanese refugees.[8] Information on the terrible problems plaguing Darfur will obviously have a profound impact in determining the solutions and rendering a judgment on the question of genocide.[9]

Third, Khartoum is being blamed for the mass murder looming over Darfur not only because of the murderous activities of the Janjaweed but also because humanitarian relief agencies insist that their efforts are being obstructed. They point to the use of red tape in delaying visas, the lack of security cooperation provided by law enforcement agencies, and general forms of bureaucratic harassment. The Sudanese have used "security" concerns to justify the obstacles placed in the paths of representatives from international organizations and humanitarian relief agencies and even foreign politicians seeking to enter the country. I proposed that the African Union, in cooperation with Sudanese representatives, be empowered to determine which humanitarian agencies should be allowed entry.

Fourth, Sudanese military leaders and politicians feared that they would be arrested for committing war crimes. That fear was only strengthened by a joint statement of European Union foreign ministers that officials of the Sudanese government and military would be "held accountable" for such crimes.[10] Various possibilities for dealing with war crimes can be discussed after peace is achieved. But for the time being, in my view, improving conditions for the IDPs in Darfur is more important than capturing and trying war criminals. Thus, my proposal—and I recognize its distasteful character—was that neither UN personnel nor humanitarian relief workers associated with any international agency should pursue arrest warrants for Sudanese nationals, even if the appropriate indictments have been provided by the International Criminal Court.[11]

Fifth, the Sudanese and the IDPs are not the only ones who have a stake in the crisis in Darfur. It has implications for the stability of nine governments whose innumerable tribes cut across national boundaries. Fighting is already taking place between different tribes, cattle growers and farmers, and private militias along the various borders separating the Sudan from its neighbors. The United Nations has placed an arms embargo of unspecified length on the Sudan, and the Sudanese leadership has stated its objection to such a ban. As things now stand, the supply of arms continues to grow, and so does the demand. It is imperative to highlight this situation and throw the glare of public opinion on it. Here again, the African Union should take the lead. It might start by sponsoring regional conferences involving political representatives, civic leaders, and respected intellectuals from different nations in the region. Other events organized by international peace organizations could publicize the problems caused by the largest sellers of military goods: China, France, Russia, and the United States. In this regard, the United States could actually play a positive role—and improve its moral standing in the international community—by implementing its own law against arms brokering rather than waiting until other nations do likewise. Articulating policies whereby the states of the region might, following Max Weber, gain a monopoly on the legitimate means of coercion would be a first step toward disarming the various tribal militias and creating the basic security that serves as the precondition for economic development. A more immediate possibility, however, is to build a climate against violence through the use of mass media, demonstrations, concerts, conferences, and the like.

This suggestion, admittedly, has a certain utopian ring to it. Participation by the most culpable states would be difficult to secure, if only because taking part would be tantamount to admitting their culpability in supplying or demanding arms. There is also the vexing question regarding who to invite and whether to include representatives from rebel groups. Furthermore, conferences, concerts, and mass media have only an indirect effect on policy. These are difficult problems to solve. Nevertheless, there is something profoundly shortsighted about refusing to think about possibilities that might help bring lasting peace to the region simply because such terrible conflict has continued for so long.

Global Darfur Day took place on September 17, 2006. Tens of thousands around the world marched against the prospect of further loss of life in the Sudan. It is easy to be cynical. Previously, there had been little concern in the West for the roughly 4 million dead in the Congo, the 1.6 million dead and displaced in Uganda, or the one in three Malawians living below the subsistence level. These events overshadow what has transpired in Darfur. But allowing the perpetration of certain humanitarian injustices in the past does not invalidate the attempt to prevent yet another disaster. World opinion ultimately helped pressure Khartoum into seeking a compromise. But this does not justify what so many of the protesters proposed as a policy. There is, indeed, something disheartening about the way Darfur was turned into a designer crisis and a media event, sentimentally oversimplified by celebrities and decent people, such as George Clooney, Mia Farrow, and Elie Wiesel, trying to do the right thing.

Clooney warned that Darfur is the new millennium's first genocide, Farrow claimed that she saw "the need for help in the refugees' eyes," and Wiesel made the Sudan yet another object of his insufferably self-righteous and selective moralizing. None of them had anything concrete to suggest, other than that sanctions should be introduced or, alternatively, that UN troops should be deployed against the Sudan. Nothing much was said about finding a compromise, forging a new approach to the crisis, or learning anything from what has transpired in Iraq. Our celebrities and mainstream progressive activists could thus be left in a terribly difficult situation. Should the United Nations prove unable to impose sanctions or intervene because of a veto introduced by China or Russia in the Security Council, the choice for Clooney and his friends would be between "doing nothing"—and perhaps watching the existing peace agreements collapse[12]—and supporting the United States in yet another high-handed gesture, if not, more ominously, another ill-advised military adventure with imperialist overtones.[13]

As things stand, ironically, the Left stands to the right of the Bush administration on the Sudan. Both Susan Rice, the top Africa official in the State Department, and Anthony Lake, national security adviser in the Clinton administration, have called for unilateral military action in Darfur and the imposition of a NATO-enforced no-fly zone over the region. Their position is not much different from that of the influential neoconservative foreign policy analyst Robert Kagan, who has argued for a U.S. invasion of the Sudan, or from that of State Department officials who favor an oil embargo and an attack by France on Sudanese military air transports. For all its bluster, so far, the Bush administration has decided only to renew existing sanctions against the Sudan for one year and hold open the option of adding new ones.

But the United States has already placed economic sanctions on nearly fifty nations—roughly a third of the states in the world community—and other powerful nations, especially China, have stepped into the breach. China is now creating a news media devoted solely to economic issues that will broadcast in Arabic twenty-four hours a day, seven days a week. I was told in Khartoum that a meeting among more than two dozen Arab and African nations and China is being planned to discuss new venues for trade. Little thought has been given to the humanitarian impact that sanctions would have on the Sudan, which ranks among the top twenty least trade-dependent states and is 139th on the United Nations' Human Misery Index. Also neglected have been the logistics and the realizable aims of twenty-two thousand UN troops—alien to the terrain and culture of Darfur—patrolling an area of 290,000 square kilometers. It is also a Western conceit to believe that UN troops will somehow prove more competent than those of the African Union, and such a substitution would surely insult African sensibilities.

UN involvement does not give intervention some kind of holy imprimatur. The insistence by Kofi Annan and others upon a "joint" UN-AU force to patrol Darfur, rather than one under the auspices of the AU, is unnecessary and unseemly. Without cooperation from Khartoum, national resistance will undoubtedly occur. Various representatives from previously warring tribes—including some from the politically powerful Zagawa and Rizgat tribes—candidly told our group that their people would engage in guerrilla actions against any "invading" force. Tens of thousands of new refugees might flee their villages, further bloating the old camps and creating scores of new ones. Even if that did not occur, however, the fighting in Sudan might touch off a regional crisis of potentially horrifying proportions.

A very different course of action remains possible. In concert with highlighting the role of the African Union and pressuring recalcitrant rebel groups to sign the Darfur Peace Agreement, an intelligent diplomatic policy—one that might counter the regional advances of China—would reject the use of economic sanctions and immediately lift those that exist. Such a policy would instead emphasize the need for microinvestment to increase the number of those with a stake in Sudanese society.[14] It would also link macroinvestment to building an infrastructure and to dollars spent by the government in repatriating the IDPs. New funding would be provided for the nearly broke Office of the United Nations High Commissioner for Refugees (UNHCR), which has repatriated more than twelve thousand IDPs, for expanding educational and cultural exchanges with the Sudan, and for fostering greater cooperation with the African Union.

Such a policy is, of course, not quite as dramatic as what another coalition of neoconservative and liberal hawks has proposed for the Sudan. No less than in Afghanistan and Iraq, but this time in a nation thirty times the size of Sierra Leone and one hundred times the size of Rwanda, they have called for foreign intervention to produce regime change under conditions that remain unexamined, and in the face of constraints that have not been taken into account. It does not matter whether their intentions are good. Should their more intemperate proposals be embraced by the United Nations or the United States, the wretched of the earth will wind up—again—bearing the consequences of military action by powerful "allies" who will surely forget about them once the costs get too high or, perhaps even worse, as soon as the next crisis comes along.

8

Conspiracy Then and Now

History, Politics, and the Anti-Semitic Imagination

The year 2005 marked the 100th anniversary of "The Protocols of the Elders of Zion."[1] Fabricated toward the end of the nineteenth century by Russian secret police agents visiting Paris—just as the first Zionist Congress was taking place in Basel in 1898—it was first published in 1905 as an appendix to a book entitled *The Great in the Small* by Sergi Nihlus. Focusing on the alleged existence of a Jewish conspiracy to take over the world, the Protocols originally had very little impact outside of sparking a few pogroms in Russia. But that changed quickly enough. Between the two world wars, the Protocols rivaled the Bible in popularity. The tract was taken seriously by any number of luminaries, including Henry Ford, who underwrote its publication in the United States, and even Winston Churchill. Auschwitz derailed its influence—for a time.

Following 9/11, the Protocols gained new prominence in the Middle East. A Pew poll taken in June 2006 showed that only 11 percent of respondents in the Islamic world believed that Muslims had something to do with the 9/11 attacks. In closed states such as Iran and Iraq, which are hothouses of gossip, rumors spread that the Jews had initiated the attack on the World Trade Center and the Pentagon and that only Jewish control over the media kept the world from realizing that "fact." The Protocols remains a hit in Iran. *The Matzah of Zion*, published in 2003 by Mustafa Tlas (the former Syrian minister of defense), is now in its eighth edition, and it offers an Arab version of the undying myth about how Jews used the blood of Christian children to bake their matzo for Passover. Then there is the forty-one-part soap opera that aired on Egyptian television, *Horse without a Horseman* (2002), in which an important episode was devoted to the supposed Jewish world conspiracy and scenes of the "Elders of Zion" melodramatically plotting their strategy. The situation has only grown worse with the American invasion of Iraq, supposedly at the behest of the Jews, and the Israeli assault on Gaza and Lebanon. Insofar as Israel has sought to identify its policies with the interests of Jews everywhere, fuel has only been added to the fire.

Anti-Semitism was always a way of interpreting social reality, and stupid interpretations make for stupid policies. Whether the new anti-Semitism has shifted from the Occident to the Orient, or whether its context or function has changed, it still employs the same method of justification. For the anti-Semite, it has never been a pedantic matter of whether any particular bigoted claim is empirically verifiable or whether a supposedly seminal tract such as the Protocols is authentic. Some even maintained that the Protocols was actually based on the minutes of the first Zionist Congress, where the language spoken was German; it never bothered any anti-Semite that the work was written in French. Empirical reality is irrelevant to a belief born of prejudice. Crucial instead is the knowledge born of "experience" or "feeling." This can never be contradicted, and for that very reason, it is sufficient.

Herein lies the initial basis for the appeal of a work like the Protocols: it turns the ignoramus into a sage in the eyes of himself and those with a prior disposition to believe what he says. There are no excuses for this form of bigoted thinking. Given the recent tirades of the president of Iran, Mahmoud Ahmadinejad, who called on Muslims to "wipe Israel off the face of the earth" and insisted that the Holocaust is a European myth imposed on the Middle East, it is vital to begin disentangling a legitimate critique of Israeli policy from plain anti-Semitism.

Works like the Protocols can serve distinctly political purposes. Appearing in imperial Russia during the democratic revolution that was sweeping the country in 1905, this tract provided a way for the aristocracy to shift blame for the uprising from its own policies and practices to an "alien" group opposed to the national complex of premodern traditions and existential social definitions associated with "throne and altar."[2] It did not matter that the Zionist movement was fragmented and in disarray following the death of Theodor Herzl in 1904. The Protocols made it possible to claim that the Revolution of 1905 was not provoked by a cruel and authoritarian theocracy ruling an economically underdeveloped land that had just been quickly defeated in the Russo-Japanese War. The Protocols made it possible to argue that the revolution was the work of an alien entity that despised Christian civilization: that alien entity was the Jews.

Anti-Semitism must be understood as more than mere prejudice. It is also an explanatory device with a social function and a political purpose. Therefore, it makes sense that the Protocols would basically disappear once the Revolution of 1905 came to an end. It also makes sense that the work's popularity would reemerge in the immediate aftermath of World War I. The end of that war brought about the collapse of four empires that had seemingly existed since time immemorial: the Russian, German, Austro-Hungarian, and Ottoman. The ancien régime had finally been demolished, and its mass base among the peasantry and the petite bourgeoisie, no less than the elites, was panicked and disoriented. These remnants of feudalism shared nothing ideologically with the proletariat and the bourgeoisie, which embraced, respectively, the socialist and liberal worldviews born of the Enlightenment. These anachronistic classes were fundamentally irrelevant to the modern production process and the secular democracies of interwar Europe, which rested on the socialist labor movement.[3] Both the premodern masses and the old elites needed not only an explanation for World War I (one that would shield them from all guilt and blame) but also a way of thinking that would existentially justify their continued salience in a world that had no use for them.

The Protocols provided that explanation and that existential self-justification: anti-Semitism became a worldview with special appeal for the "losers" in the development of modernity. Not every opponent of the Enlightenment legacy became a Nazi, of course, and not every peasant, petit bourgeois, or aristocrat became an anti-Semite. But there existed what Max Weber called an "elective affinity" (*Wahlverwandschaft*) between counter-Enlightenment thought and a rising fascist-Nazi movement, as well as between premodern groups threatened by modernity and anti-Semitism. In the worldview of this right-wing revolutionary movement, which would seemingly always have these premodern groups as its mass base, the primary issue was the threat to Christian—or Aryan[4]—civilization posed by an anti-Christian or "alien" segment of society identified with rationalism and modernity. This alien entity, again, could only be the Jews, who had not merely rejected but also murdered the Savior, and whose nefarious plans were made plain in the Protocols. Jews and their agents were seen as manipulating the proletariat *and* the bourgeoisie, propagating socialism *and* liberalism, fostering social justice *and* civil liberties, introducing Bolshevik dictatorship *and* parliamentary democracy.[5] The Protocols, indeed, had the virtue of crystallizing every opponent of the anti-Semite into a single enemy.

Rediscovered and used by the "Whites" against the "Reds" during the civil war that immediately followed the Russian Revolution of 1917, the tract was brought to the capitals of Europe by reactionary émigrés. Alfred Rosenberg, who introduced the Protocols to the young Nazi movement and later became Hitler's court philosopher, was among them.[6] The pamphlet peddled by Rosenberg and others like him had particular salience for the Germans, who had experienced the destruction of their empire apparently without warning. News from the battlefields was severely censored, and by 1918, the old elites were already promulgating the myth that the army had never been defeated at the front. Germany had instead been "stabbed in the back," and the Protocols made it clear who had held the knife.

Such an explanation profoundly changed the understanding of World War I. The prewar elites were absolved of responsibility for causing the catastrophe, and a foundation was created for an alignment between them and the new proponents of the "conservative revolution," or the burgeoning fascist Right, with its militant ideals deriving from what Ernst Jünger called "the brotherhood of the trenches." The Protocols linked the old romantic nationalism of the nineteenth century with the neoromantic, and ultimately racist, brand of the twentieth century. The pamphlet provided what Georges Sorel termed a "myth": a sense of peril, a motivation for action, a justification for violence, and, perhaps above all, a heroic self-understanding for these two wings of an international reactionary movement united by a resistance to the heirs of the Enlightenment and the harbingers of modernity. There is, indeed, nothing mysterious about the popularity enjoyed by the Protocols during the interwar period.

Anti-Semitism was socially acceptable almost everywhere in Europe: *Volkskunde,* or the equivalent, was taught in schools;

the higher reaches of society were closed to Jews; and most nations resented that these former ghetto dwellers were entering the public sphere. Virtually every Continental nation faced the same conflicts over modernity between the advocates of liberalism and socialism, on the one hand, and the reactionaries of the old and the new Right, on the other. Usually forgotten due to the extreme nationalism preached by the Nazis is the cooperation between the Action Française, the Spanish Falange, and Opus Dei, as well as fascist groups in Italy, Hungary, Romania, and elsewhere. International publishing consortiums, often supported by important industrialists such as Hugo Stinnes, linked them as surely as various publishing enterprises linked the socialists and the communists of different nations. The popularity of the Protocols, then, was that they met the needs of an international situation in which the traditional Right and the new fascist Right were facing roughly similar conditions throughout Europe.

To be sure, the Protocols provided no economic, political, or organizational views that might bind traditional conservatism with revolutionary fascism. But the tract did insist on what Ernst Cassirer termed a "mytho-poetic" rather than a rational or scientific way of understanding social reality. It drew a line in the sand between the supporters of the Enlightenment legacy and its critics. The Protocols insisted that, like the Indian god Vishnu, with his countless tentacles, the Jew controlled all the institutions, parties, and media associated with what merely *appeared* to be the contradictory forces of modernity. The pamphlet claimed that, in reality, modernity was unified; a single alien agency was at work, but it lurked in the shadows. Anti-Semites would make the most of these claims during the interwar years when Walther Rathenau, a Jewish industrialist and the foreign minister of Germany during the Weimar Republic, stated (critically) the phrase that became a famous slogan: "300 men control the future of Europe." Empirical investigation was therefore unnecessary and insufficient for discovering the "hidden hand" manipulating events. Intuition and experience were required for gleaning the alien agent of social destruction, and these intuitive qualities were naturally seen as belonging only to the most *irrationally conscious* representatives of the Christian—or, ultimately, Aryan—"community" (*Volksgemeinshaft*).[7]

Anticipating the future, the Protocols made it clear that all things are possible: world war and world domination. The Jews had brought about the catastrophe faced by Europeans in the 1920s and 1930s, and, given the intelligence of their enemy, the tract suggested that anti-Semites must be willing to react with the same ruthlessness, the same insistence on ethnic loyalty, the same stealth, and the same manipulation of the media and the public sphere. Resistance against "the Jew" could therefore be justified by psychological projection. Through a combination of myth and prejudice, the supposed violence, lying, and manipulation of the Jews became the very activities in which the anti-Semites actually engaged. The lie thus became the truth. Heinrich Himmler put the matter well when he noted a few years after World War I that the Protocols "explains everything and . . . tells us whom we should fight the next time."

It is somewhat of an exaggeration to suggest that the Protocols offered "a warrant for genocide."[8] Genocide is not broached in the tract, and even those like Richard Wagner, who embraced the most extreme nineteenth-century forms of anti-Semitism, had no sense of the practical implications of their theoretical ravings. The Holocaust can only be considered sui generis. No movement and no writer, with the possible exception of Kafka, anticipated anything like Auschwitz. What the Protocols did offer, however, was an articulated understanding of what I have termed the "chameleon effect." This means that the Jew changes shape to fit whatever enemy of society is required: the Jew is the liberal, the socialist, the communist, the avant-gardist, the homosexual, and so forth. Just as the Jew can take any form, any Jew can be a member of the conspiracy. And since the conspiracy is invisible, even the most innocent Jew must be presumed guilty. The extent to which the chameleon effect operates is the extent to which anti-Semitism really informs a reactionary worldview. In Germany, where (for complex reasons) the chameleon effect was most radical, there was ultimately (using the phrase of Hannah Arendt) no "place" for any Jew in society, and in this sense, genocide became a logical necessity.

Hegel liked to speak about the "cunning" of history, whereby consequences transform intentions and intentions turn into their opposite. Anti-Semitism is a case in point. Auschwitz rendered anti-Semitism socially unacceptable in Europe and actually forged the bonds among Jews that had been lacking prior to World War II. Once the dimensions of the Holocaust became public, which is precisely why modern bigots stress its denial, the connection between anti-Semitic theory and its hideous practical implications was inescapable. Outside the Middle East, anti-Semitism is no longer taught in schools; it lacks a new literature, it is bereft of an articulated chameleon effect, and it lacks a secure mass base. In the Western democracies, at least, no party or organization that embraces anti-Semitism as its dominant ideology has a serious chance at taking power. To deny the difference between the way anti-Semitism was practiced in the interwar period and its practice today leaves the individual wandering in (to borrow another phrase from Hegel) "the night in which all cows are black."

To insist that liberal critics of Israeli policies are really self-hating Jews, or that much of the world is again ganging up on the helpless Palestinian victim, or that anti-Semitism has remained unchanged is both wrong and unhelpful. Without a sense of context, combating the contemporary bigot becomes much more difficult. The Jew was the victim in the 1920s and 1930s, just as the Jew had been the victim throughout the preceding centuries. Jews were subjugated in a Christian world that remained enthralled with the feudal traditions of throne and altar. Tolerance was often less a matter of law than of whimsy, and Jews lived in fear of reactionary institutions and paranoid religious outbursts by the Christian community. Jews were fragmented but seen as unified, ostracized but seen as invasive, powerless but seen as omnipotent. In short, the fear of a Jewish conspiracy whose goal was world conquest lacked any trace of empirical justification, and the anti-Semitic portrait of the Jew had nothing to do with living, breathing Jews.

Today, however, the situation has changed. Jews no longer lack their own state, lobbyists to represent their interests, or a fundamental unity. In all the Western democracies, interest groups are working on issues of concern to a Jewish constituency, and Jews are entrenched in modern society. Terrible things still occur. A cemetery is still desecrated here and there; now and then a Jew is beaten up on his way home from synagogue; or some crackpot or another denies the Holocaust. But the police are usually on the case, and grievances are generally addressed. Anti-Semitic utterances are instantly condemned by most of the international community, and in Western nations, even "salon" anti-Semitism is considered a vulgar holdover from times past.

Anti-Semitism is no longer what it was. Although its remnants can still be found in Russia and Poland and in the ravings of the Far Right in Europe, the old bigoted ideology is now most prevalent in the Middle East: the site of the Israeli-Palestinian conflict. Jews may wish to view themselves as the victims of history, but Israel cannot. It has the fourth largest army in the world and is clearly the strongest military power in the Middle East; in addition to dozens of favorable arms sales, it received around $100 billion in foreign aid and other grants and loans between 1949 and 2006.[9] Israel has mostly been victorious on the battlefield; it has expelled inhabitants living in what are known as the Occupied Territories, it oversees 5.5 million Palestinians living in fifty-nine refugee camps, and it is making the most of borders that are arbitrarily imposed and not clearly defined. There is something profoundly disingenuous in comparisons of anti-Semitism today and its expression in times past. Embracing such comparisons undermines critical thinking, fosters a reverse racism, paves the way for political manipulation, and—perhaps above all—insults the memory of people who paid the highest price for their beliefs and truly suffered under the yoke of bigotry.

Anti-Semitism still exists; however, it exists in a new and very different context. To be sure, this form of prejudice can still be used to displace discontent and distract attention from the failings of politicians and their governments. But bigotry against Jews has also become interwoven with the barbarous treatment of the Palestinians; attempts by right-wing Zionists and religious zealots to create a "Greater Israel," along with their incredible alliance with the Christian Right in the United States; and Israel's willingness to support reactionary regimes in world affairs and its uncritical embrace of U.S. foreign policy.[10] For all the talk about peace and security, Israel has been creating more settlements on the West Bank—populated primarily by fanatical Zionists and religious zealots—and implementing policies akin to apartheid with respect to its own growing Arab citizenry. The Middle East thus provides a very different context for anti-Semitism and imbues this ideology with a different set of symbolic meanings than it had in Europe.

It is important to remember that the Protocols set up an unqualified conflict between Jews and non-Jews without reference to context or conditions. This tract had little use for rational argumentation or empirical evidence, relying instead on intuition and myth. It was, in the first instance, an attempt to clamp down on discourse, and because writings like the Protocols arbitrarily identify the enemy of "civilization" with a set of stereotypes, anti-Semitic assumptions can actually be embraced by Jews themselves.[11] It is completely legitimate to condemn genuine expressions of anti-Semitism that are based on evil stereotypes and hysterical paranoia. But it is another matter to portray every mention of the Protocols as a step toward the emergence of a new Hitler and every criticism of Israeli policy as an expression of anti-Semitism. Some Jewish zealots see a conflict stemming from time immemorial between the Jews and the goyim; it is often said among Jews (though usually in private) that the anti-Semites have dominated them for two thousand years, and now that the Jews have power, there is no reason to give an inch. The retreat into "racial" or tribal thinking is a logical consequence.

Jews thereby become defined by what they should oppose. What results is not merely a form of anti-Semitic blowback but also a more subtle resentment of the need for "permission to narrate" events in the Middle East from any perspective other than those acceptable to professional supporters of the Israeli state.[12] Such a stance is self-defeating. It calls on Jews to embrace untenable myths and assumptions and thereby impairs their ability to understand the criticisms directed against them. New research suggests that the once firmly held belief that Israel was the product of a "people without a land [finding] a land without a people" was a myth from the beginning; the same is true of the old notion of a founding in which the original settlers were peacefully removed from their land and an overwhelming Arab force united by its bigotry was valiantly defeated by the "miracle" of Jewish national unity.[13] Finally, less persuasive today is the attempt to invoke the memory of the Holocaust to justify every reactionary twist and turn of Israeli policy—if only because the Palestinians played no role in it. As the world grows larger, as other atrocities take center stage, and as the survivors pass on, the philosophical and historical meaning and symbolism of the Holocaust need to change along with established patterns of thinking and plain ethnocentric prejudices that inhibit the emergence of a new discussion.[14]

Dealing with ongoing anti-Semitic beliefs in a Jewish plan for world conquest, or in a Jew-inspired invasion of Iraq,[15] requires admitting that Jews are no longer in the ghetto or an oppressed minority. It also calls for recognizing that anti-Semitism is entangled in a political crisis rendered more difficult by the way Palestinians can be considered (using a phrase from Edward Said) "the victim of a victim." Disentangling genuine prejudice from a legitimate critique of Israel's imperialist ambitions should be the aim of all progressive or critical inquiry into the problem of anti-Jewish bigotry. It would, of course, be naïve to expect anti-Jewish prejudice to disappear even if a new Palestinian state were created and even if the United States were to withdraw support from corrupt regimes such as Saudi Arabia and change its policies in the Middle East. Conquering prejudice is not a mechanical exercise, and its success is not a foregone conclusion. The suffering endured by generations of Palestinians, by those who experienced the Israeli invasion of Lebanon in 1982, and by others in the Middle East will leave an arguably ineradicable residue. Nevertheless, it makes sense to believe that anti-Semitism will diminish at least somewhat if Israel changes its imperialist policies.

Works like the Protocols, however, undermine any such effort. The seemingly immutable struggle between Christian and Jew becomes extrapolated in a new context as the struggle between Arab and Jew—to the detriment of both. Prejudice makes it impossible to differentiate between progressive and regressive tendencies within the world community and the Israeli state.[16] By the same token, it enables Jews to avoid choosing between the imperatives of a democratic, nonimperialist state and the current regime. Anti-Semitism thereby subverts the ability to develop a sensible politics even as it renders any form of reconciliation impossible. Works like the Protocols—now one hundred years old—still play into the hands of the most reactionary elements in both Israeli and Arab society, thereby guaranteeing a further downward spiral. Such works remain the crutch for the most dangerous elements in politics: intellectual laziness and ideological fanaticism.

9

Incendiary Images

Blasphemous Cartoons, Cosmopolitan Responsibility, and Critical Engagement

> Culture is only true when implicitly critical, and the mind which forgets this revenges itself in the critics it breeds.
>
> Theodor W. Adorno

Symbolic politics cannot be divorced from practical politics. This is true not merely when dealing with clashes between East and West, Muslim and Christian, but also with conflicts between any traditional religious community and the liberal, secular world of modernity. Such themes run through much of my work, and like many others, I was appalled and fascinated when, in February 2006, a right-wing Danish newspaper published twelve cartoons satirizing the prophet Muhammad and insulting the entire Islamic community. As they were reprinted again and again, demonstrations—some violent and some peaceful—spread rapidly throughout Europe and many nations in Africa, Asia, and the Middle East. Islamic fanatics lost no time in manipulating the situation to legitimate their own intolerance. No less than the anti-immigrant Right, they wished to destroy the possibility of cross-cultural understanding and foster a "clash of civilizations" through the violence they instigated. The fanatical proponents of symbolic politics on both sides of the barricades presented a mirror image of each other, even as they were opposed by the cosmopolitan elements within their own communities.

The prospect of an increasingly interdependent world calls for linking free speech with a sense of responsibility concerning its exercise. But this does not mean endorsing a form of dogmatism masquerading as cultural sensitivity that is willing to countenance criticism only when it is directed against others. The recent protests of French Muslims against a new production of Voltaire's play *Fanaticism or Mahomet the Prophet* (1748) were just as appalling as the Jewish community's initial responses to the premiere of a play about young activist Rachel Corrie, who was killed by an Israeli bulldozer while trying to prevent the destruction of a Palestinian home. Fanatics have always equated the word with the deed. Today, more than ever, it is incumbent upon progressives to both defend and expand free speech and civil liberties and, at the same time, insist on legal sanctions against violent acts of bigotry. The choice cannot be between those who offer platitudes about free speech and those who use cultural sensitivity as a shield against criticism of the violence they employ. Actions such as those that led to the banning of a gay pride parade in Jerusalem—actions that had the support of leaders from all the major religious communities—can only create a climate of constraint. It thus becomes the task of the Left to restore the original critical aim behind all civil liberties by resurrecting their relevance for the "outsider," emphasizing their connection to demands for public accountability, and highlighting their resistance to the arbitrary exercise of power.

The political cartoon has a long history. Some of it is bright and noble: Goya satirized the Catholic Inquisition with his wonderful *capprichios;* Daumier held up the mirror by which French society could see itself in the latter part of the nineteenth century; George Grosz scandalized "good society" with his sketches of the decadent rich and the despondent victims of World War I; Art Spiegelman dared to use images of rats and vermin employed by the Nazi propagandists to depict the lives of Jews amid the Holocaust, while his teacher, the late Will Eisner, narrated and criticized "The Protocols of the Elders of Zion" in *The Plot.*[1] Each of these artists used the cartoon to foster reflection, expose the excesses of the powerful, and build a feeling of humanity denied. The best of them evidenced a sense of critical engagement, love of freedom, and cosmopolitan responsibility. Their work needed the protection accorded by civil liberties because it dared to contest the reigning belief system and the arrogance of power.

But the tradition of the political cartoon also has another historical tendency. It can be found in the portrait of a lecherous Voltaire sodomizing his niece; the depiction of "little Sambo" and the slaves who love their slavery; the pornographic treatment of Jews in the pages of the Nazi rag *Der Sturmer,* edited by the notorious Julius Streicher; or the caricatures of Gandhi and the victims of colonialism who deserve the exploitation they get. Cartoons such as these undermine reflection, toady to the powerful, and rub out any sense of a common humanity. They disfigure what Emmanuel Levinas called "the face of the other" and, when caught in the act, plead that they are "testing the limits" and cynically insist on their right to free speech. This tradition defines the artistic context for the contemporary political cartoons of the prophet Muhammad with a bomb in his turban, and the others with like-minded stereotypical and racist images, that provoked the rage of Muslims during February 2006.

Jyllands-Poste, a reactionary Danish tabloid, first published the twelve insulting cartoons in September 2005. Haughtily aware of their civil liberties, ignoring the tensions within a newly multicultural society and the cultural vulnerabilities of Muslim immigrants, the Danish editors said that they never would have published the cartoons "had they only known" what violence they would unleash. Part of the problem stems from a general lack of knowledge of the "other" that reigns in both the Occident and the Orient. The strength of such ignorance is commensurate with the weakness of any sense of cosmopolitan responsibility. Nevertheless, there is something disingenuous about all this.

When I was writing my book *A Rumor about the Jews: Anti-Semitism, Conspiracy, and the Protocols of Zion,*[2] it occurred to me that few readers would actually have read the Protocols. The question became whether I should include selections from this bigoted fabrication or not. Including selections would obviously mean publicizing a work of anti-Semitic rubbish; possibly offending a number of Jews; and, because the book was set to appear simultaneously in English and German, perhaps running afoul of the hate speech legislation in the *Bundesrepublik.* Ultimately, I decided that including these offensive selections was necessary for pedagogical purposes. I was willing to deal with the fact that good pedagogical intentions can lead to unfortunate consequences and that one cannot know in advance what kind of impact these selections might have.

None of these considerations, however, applies to the European editors who published the cartoons. There was no pedagogical purpose involved. It does not take a genius to figure out that lampooning the Prophet is a particularly grievous blasphemy to the adherents of Islam. Any reasonably intelligent person today would know that. No less than Jews, Muslims consider iconography blasphemous and the depiction of their Prophet an insult. Even if the original publication of the cartoons had been driven by a pedagogical intent, it was unnecessary for other editors of other papers to reprint them. The cartoons could have been described, and the original Web site could have been referenced so that readers who desired to do so could sneak a peek. This was not simply a free-speech issue; it also involved the hypocrisy of the sensation-seeking commercial media and a lack of concern for the public welfare. Islamic demonstrations against the cartoons broke out roughly four months after their initial publication—only after other conservative and anti-immigrant papers had reprinted the images, and mullahs in Europe and elsewhere decided to turn them into a cause célèbre. The cartoons were used not to edify and inform but to sell newspapers and build ratings. It was the incessant reprinting of the cartoons that fanned the flames and turned their publication into a deadly provocation.

The racist intent behind publishing the cartoons was evident from the start, and satirizing the Prophet soon led to a variety of other stunts. A group of Iranian soccer players were depicted as suicide bombers. A right-wing Italian politician, Roberto Calderoli, paraded in front of television cameras with an offensive cartoon emblazoned on his T-shirt, sparking deadly demonstrations against the Italian consulate in Libya. The Danish People's Party has gained support from the controversy unleashed by *Jyllands-Poste,* and it is no accident that its cultural editor, Flemming Rose, views the outrage directed against the cartoons as a "wake-up call" for the Danes. Rose, an ardent admirer of the neoconservative and ultra-Zionist writer Daniel Pipes, claimed that "Danish people are no longer willing to pay taxes to help support someone called Ali who comes from a country with a different language and culture that is 5,000 miles away."[3] The backlash is evident everywhere in Europe, and in France, a new piece of legislation proposes making it more difficult for low-income immigrants to bring in their relatives. Indeed, those most outraged by the response to the cartoons are the same people who published or supported publishing them in the first place.[4]

Since 9/11, there has been a tendency to identify Islam

as the enemy in the "war on terror." Western leaders have, admittedly, tried to draw distinctions between the majority of believers in Islam and its fanatical minority.[5] But this attempt has foundered on the reef of right-wing media demagoguery, the constant saber rattling of Western nations in the Middle East, and a general privileging of Israeli interests. Despite the tensions, most citizens in the western democracies are not radically at odds with the bulk of the Islamic community.[6] All too predictably, however, a small circle of Islamic fanatics pounced on the cartoons to justify their own fanaticism. The breakdown of good faith was precisely what the Islamic radicals sought to bring about through the violence they both fostered and manipulated.

The Danish imam Abu Laban fanned the flames of anger by distributing cartoons depicting the prophet Muhammad as a pig and a pedophile that had supposedly been "received" by Muslims in Denmark.[7] Iranian president Mahmoud Ahmadinejad blamed the cartoons on a Zionist "plot" to revenge the electoral victory of Hamas in Palestine. Syria played up the cartoons and approved mass demonstrations that deflected from other issues such as its involvement in Lebanon and domestic repression. In Pakistan, where an "errant" American missile had killed many members of a large village, the cartoons sparked riots directed against the secular government of General Pervez Musharraf and his alliance with the United States. These protests were generated from both the top down and the bottom up. Many took place in Europe, but understandably, most occurred in states with a Muslim majority or a sizable Muslim minority, such as Afghanistan, Pakistan, Bangladesh, India, Sri Lanka, Kenya, Indonesia, and the Sudan.

Flags were burned, official apologies were demanded (and refused), and protesters set fire to Danish and other Western embassies throughout the Middle East. Death threats were made to the editors of papers that carried the cartoons. Nine people were killed in Libya, ten in Afghanistan, and more than one hundred in Nigeria, where, in response to Muslim attacks on churches and Catholic shops, Christian mobs revenged themselves on their neighbors. Cries of "Strike, strike, bin Laden" could be heard in Khartoum, Islamabad, and Gaza. Israel and the United States were excoriated, and millions of dollars in property was destroyed. In various places, demonstrators numbered in the tens of thousands. Ignored were the peaceful demonstrations and the voices of reason in the Muslim community—among them that of the Ayatollah Ali Sistani, leader of the Shiites in Iraq—who denounced the violence. It was not simply the number of demonstrators but their vehemence that sold the papers.

The mainstream media on both sides of the great divide were irresponsible in their presentation of the controversy. One is ostensibly "free" but dependent on the market; the other is controlled by authoritarian figures who can only benefit from the displacement of resentment. Each turned its enemy into a stereotype and espoused a symbolic politics that permits no compromise. What was popularly considered a vindication for the "clash of civilizations" is better understood as a conflict between fanatics who are ignorant of the "other." And these fanatics are opposed by cosmopolitan voices within their own respective communities in both the East and the West.

Highlighting free speech without referring to the moral responsibility for its exercise—a cosmopolitan responsibility in the face of increasing globalization and a growing interface between radically different cultures—can only render liberal ideals abstract and produce what Herbert Marcuse termed "repressive tolerance." There has always been a tension between the imperatives of law and the dictates of morality, and it is perverse to discuss one without reference to the other.

Maintaining a commitment to free speech does *not* imply that any given media outlet must accept any piece of news or literature that comes across the desk of an editor. It is also not simply a matter of shouting "fire" in a crowded building. Editors routinely reject manuscripts, and newspapers need not accept advertisements from neo-Nazis. Consensus determines the particularly "legitimate" range of political debate and criticism in the United States. Even sports pundits have been fired for making relatively timid racial remarks or insulting one specific community or another. Most European nations have laws against "hate speech." Britain, in fact, still has a blasphemy law that criminalizes defaming the Christian God. Austria imprisoned the Holocaust denier David Irving, and the most famous Holocaust denier, Ernst Zundel, was indicted on fourteen charges in Germany.[8] The mullahs are surely correct when they note that denying the Holocaust or inciting anti-Semitism is usually considered a crime, while insulting Islam and its Prophet is viewed as a legitimate expression of free speech.

Still, throughout this preposterous controversy, the outraged Muslim fanatics have been as cynical as their opponents in exploiting an opportunity, and too rarely do they question their own reliance on a double standard. They say nothing about the government-sponsored publication of works such as the Protocols or the use of vile anti-Semitic textbooks throughout the Middle East. Such activity only further poisons the political atmosphere. Attempts by the right-wing European media to inflame anti-immigrant feelings do not justify attempts by Islamic fanatics and bigots to intensify anti-Semitic and anti-Western sentiments. Responding to these hateful anti-Islamic cartoons by placing an $11 million bounty on the head of the Danish cartoonists or creating a contest to award a prize to the best caricature of the Holocaust also shows a dearth of emotional maturity and cosmopolitan responsibility. Such posturing self-indulgence is indefensible and inexcusable: the victim again becomes defined by what he should oppose. It is best to recall Gandhi's observation that responding to every grievance with the invocation of "an eye for an eye" will ultimately leave the whole world blind.

Two options present themselves: legislation that criminalizes the denial of the Holocaust or the defaming of Christianity must be extended to include Islam, or all such legislation must be wiped off the books. The problem with the first position is that racism would be driven underground, and its purveyors might well turn into martyrs. Censoring critics of religious faith could easily allow reactionary religious institutions to insulate themselves from any type of meaningful criticism. What is more, historically, disastrous forms of blowback have resulted every time the Left has sought to constrain civil liberties. With respect to the second position, however, expanding free speech in legal terms does little to address the issue of cosmopolitan or moral responsibility regarding its exercise, and there is even less concern with abused sensibilities that might produce violence. Adherents of this stance are content to insist, with political and legal theorist Ronald Dworkin, that "religion must be tailored to democracy, not the other way around."[9]

That is true enough. But the way to begin is by recognizing the difference between the word and the deed. "Hate speech" is not the same as a "hate crime." Commitment to expanding the realm of discourse is a fundamental element of the liberal legacy and the best progressive political traditions. But this does not invalidate the need for simple politeness and civility, particularly in a potentially incendiary situation. There is also no reason why the commitment to free speech cannot be linked with legal sanctions against violent acts of prejudice. Special legislation against hate crimes was passed in the United States in the aftermath of the 1960s, and it had a profound impact on those engaged in discriminatory practices directed against people of color, gays, and other "outsiders."

It is imperative that progressives move beyond the present discursive impasse. In the aftermath of the cartoon controversy, free speech and civil liberties are now seen as part of the arsenal available to supposedly innocent right-wing editors in Europe to defend provincial and racist provocations. Meanwhile, traditionalists and fundamentalist proponents of Islam insist on protection from satire and criticism for themselves—though not for adherents to other religions—in the name of human dignity. Put another way, hypocritical beneficiaries of liberalism and equally hypocritical manipulators of religious faith have each gotten their fair share of the ideological profits from this debate. The endless platitudes converge, and for all the moral posturing, they expose a position in the West that is content to let sleeping dogs lie. Little time has been wasted on those brave newspaper editors in Jordan and Yemen whose willingness to publish the cartoons not only tested the theocratic institutions and moral boundaries of their communities but also cost them their jobs, their standing, and perhaps even their lives. It is always easy for the self-righteous to forget that context counts when talking about the exercise of liberty. Those who really do think differently have—as usual—been abandoned.

Rational radicals in the future will have to confront not only a new form of repressive tolerance but also the repressive manipulation of "sensitivity" by those who are seemingly unaware that meaningful free speech has always had a bite. By the same token, critical thinkers will have to develop criteria for making moral—not simply legal—judgments about the role, the limits, and the possibilities of free expression. It is not enough to let the hand-wringing defenders of the "liberal" state and the provincial upholders of "illiberal" religions continue baiting each other forever. The partisans of radical thinking must break the deadlock by beginning to reconsider the *positive* aims that critique should serve.

Caught between one imperative not to destroy free speech and another imperative not to offend anyone by its exercise, the work of genuine radicals will become more difficult. They will increasingly have to justify their assault on the status quo in terms different from those employed by the phony rebels—the "shock jocks" and their ilk—who identify freedom with license. The controversy produced by these incendiary images has made it necessary to provide a new cosmopolitan meaning for the notion of liberty. That is a stiff challenge. It is, however, one that each generation of genuine radicals has had to face, and it is unavoidable today for those who would foster the cause of freedom.

10

Of Reason and Faith

On the Former Cardinal Josef Ratzinger

I felt a strange twinge of delight when Cardinal Josef Ratzinger was elected pope on April 24, 2005. That was because I had had the privilege of meeting him at a party in 1973 while I was studying at the University of Tübingen on a Fulbright scholarship. The future Pope Benedict XVI had taught theology there before moving to the University of Regensburg in 1972. Of course, there is no reason why he should remember me, but I certainly remember him. Professor Ratzinger made a distinct impression on me with his penetrating eyes and sober demeanor. He was already known as a brilliant theologian whose conservatism had originally been fueled by political and cultural disillusionment with the student movement of 1968. The pope remains adamant about the need to counteract the empowering of reason at the expense of faith, secularism at the expense of spirituality, and the Enlightenment heritage at the expense of religious ritual.

This is the legacy of modernity and what might be termed "Enlightenment fundamentalism"—that is, a basic reliance on the secular, liberal, and critical heritage of the eighteenth century—which some consider the principal danger to Western societies. But the current pontiff never lacked a sense of nuance. He has called Roman Catholicism the finest blend of reason and faith, even though he has also tended to highlight the "prepolitical," or religious, roots of Europe and the need to build a more doctrinally unified Catholic Church. His speech of September 13, 2006, which included comments about the Prophet Muhammad and jihad (culled from an obscure Byzantine emperor)[1] that insulted the Islamic community, may have been intended only to challenge irrational terrorists hiding under the cloak of religion, but it also served the practical purpose of inspiring provincial forces within his own religious community. "In Pursuit of Peace," an article that appeared in 2004 when the pope was still a cardinal, provides an exceptional insight into his general outlook.[2]

My own views on the Enlightenment and its impact are very different.[3] That the Enlightenment legacy has been unable to eradicate provincialism, imperialism, capitalist exploitation, and religious intolerance speaks to the way its radical project—along with its socialist implications—has been truncated. The Enlightenment ethos, in my view, has inspired virtually every major political struggle for social justice and human rights. Its major philosophers were all opponents of dogmatism and, whatever their own prejudices, the arbitrary exercise of power. I also think that the most radically democratic societies are those that have most radically divorced church from state and that the real danger to humanity has never been science, let alone reason, but the political choices concerning its employment. The genuine threat has always appeared when myth and intuition were invoked as criteria of judgment, when reason was denied, when tradition was embraced for its own sake, and when religious dogma dominated the public sphere—that is, when intolerance was strongest and when the possibilities for ideological manipulation from above, coupled with the unleashing of the passions from below, were greatest. Uncritical faith rather than reasoned reflection, myth rather than science, obedience rather than critical speculation, and prejudice rather than knowledge remain the enemies of freedom.

"In Pursuit of Peace" opens with the future pontiff's reflections on D-day and the subsequent liberation of Europe from the Nazis. What resulted was an unparalleled period of peace and prosperity whose framers (somewhat arbitrarily chosen), according to Ratzinger, derived their political motivations from their Christian beliefs. With the help of the Marshall Plan and the military backing of the United States, Western Europe squared off against the communist bloc. Ratzinger is right when he notes that the lie born of "ideological tyranny" predominated under the communists as surely as it had predominated under the Nazis. Nevertheless, the world looks different depending on which side of the North-South divide one is standing.

Leaders of all the "great powers" that built the postwar compact were complicit—some perhaps more and others perhaps less than their predecessors and successors—in shaping the nightmare of poverty and instability that still hovers over the once colonized world. Even the greatest figures of the struggle against totalitarianism—Winston Churchill, Franklin Roosevelt, and Harry Truman—supported crass imperialist exploits, compromised with tyrants, and justified the creation or use of nuclear weapons. None of these men have the same aura in India, Latin America, and Asia that they have in the West. It is instructive that, with the agreement of the United States, Churchill specifically exempted British colonial possessions from the principles of the Atlantic Charter.

Ratzinger views the problems of the non-Western world as deriving from its inability to maintain the rule of law, which would enable different groups to live together, and its mixture of cynical self-interest and an abuse of "faith" that ultimately inhibits the exercise of conscience. Recourse to the terror unleashed on September 11, 2001, was a logical consequence of such religious perversions, and according to the cardinal, the dangers have only grown worse since biological and nuclear weapons are no longer the preserve of Western nations alone. Here, the double standard becomes apparent once again. Ratzinger never mentions the devastating impact of imperialism or the bombing of Hiroshima and Nagasaki—a glaring omission. He also evidences little sense of the bitter irony of the United States lecturing the once colonized world about nuclear proliferation while leading all nations in the sale of weapons and reserving for itself alone the right to engage in a preemptive strike whenever its leaders feel the need to do so.

But the "clash of civilizations" between the West and Islam is not the cardinal's primary focus. It is instead the growing "pathological" embrace of either "reason" or "religion" and the need to restore a proper balance between the two: more secular reason in the Orient and more religious faith in the Occident. On first blush, therefore, his article exhibits a reasonableness that is difficult to deny. But there is also something odd, and abstract, about considering the existence of too much fanaticism and repression as essentially equivalent to the existence of too much tolerance and freedom. His primary concern is with the West and the way the "good" is becoming subordinated to the "useful." The more truth becomes identified with objectivity and the testability of scientific claims, according to Ratzinger, the more morality and religion will turn into matters of purely "subjective" belief or opinion. Such is the legacy of scientific rationality, or a form of uncritical positivism that has often been conflated with Enlightenment philosophy.

Ratzinger's argument owes an impressive debt to the thinking of contrasting philosophers such as Martin Heidegger and

Max Horkheimer. No less than they, however, Ratzinger forgets that the unfettered ability of science to question authority has historically been intertwined with the emergence of political democracy. He is also mistaken in suggesting that (neo)positivism implies merely the rule of the majority (*Mehrheitsprinzip*) rather than the right of the minority to contest received opinions—precisely because truth is deemed provisional and inherently falsifiable. For this reason, whatever purely philosophical criticisms one might level against them, most of the major positivist philosophers were political liberals. Although it is unfair to lump all critics of positivism together, it is telling that the attack on positivism is a characteristic of all totalitarian regimes.[4] In the same vein, it is interesting that the nineteenth-century socialist parties that identified ideologically with a positivistic, deterministic, and scientific Marxism produced the first mass democratic organizations in Europe, the most enthusiastic supporters of the interwar republics, and the most principled opponents of both communist and fascist totalitarianism.

To make his point about the danger of embracing either faith or reason, the cardinal contrasts the irrationalism of Hitler with the ultrarationality of Marxism. But the fact is that communism jettisoned the historical logic, the rationality, and the "science" of Marxism. Willing to seize power in an underdeveloped nation where the proletariat was a tiny minority, Leninism rested on a thoroughly romantic politics of the will. Thus, it made sense for Antonio Gramsci—a stalwart of Leninism and a founder of the Italian Communist Party—to call the Russian Revolution a "revolution against *Das Kapital.*" Unconcerned with accountable institutions, insistent that any historical constraint can be overcome, and arbitrary in its designation of enemies, the unqualified faith in the party soon turned into an unqualified faith in its leader, whose obiter dicta supplanted any coherent theoretical perspective. What became the Left totalitarian trajectory, as it developed from Lenin to Stalin, perfectly reflected the Right totalitarian development from Mussolini to Hitler. In short, it is not the case that the Right was romantic and irrational while the Left was overly scientific and rational. Ratzinger is also mistaken about Pol Pot, who may have exemplified the most extreme version of romantic left-wing irrationalism with his willingness to sacrifice roughly a third of his people in the insane desire to re-create an agricultural golden age supposedly lost in the mists of time. There is a reason for the title of what remains the most telling explanation for the appeal of communism: "the god that failed."[5]

There is, by the same token, something profoundly exaggerated about Ratzinger's claim that "Christian belief" produced the worldly states where all could live in peace. The ghetto was not exactly a Jewish invention, and the "white man's burden," which promoted Christian missionary activity, did not exactly help foster peace in Africa. The Catholic Church, for the most part, opposed the democratic revolutions of the eighteenth and nineteenth centuries and consistently sought to block republican attempts to integrate Jews and Muslims into the everyday life of European civil society. What makes the cardinal's preamble about D-day so relevant for understanding the political role of religion is, ironically, that the church made peace with democracy and the civil rights of non-Christians—to the extent it has—only after the Second World War. During the Dreyfus affair, the rise of Mussolini, the Weimar Republic, the Spanish civil war, and the triumph of Hitler, its lot was cast with the authoritarian Right. That was also the case in Latin America and other colonial territories, even though a minority of Catholic activists and priests identified with "liberation theology" (which the Catholic establishment consistently criticized) and put forth a valiant resistance against authoritarian dictators and their imperialist allies. To be sure, the church played an important role in the struggle against communist totalitarianism, and Pope John Paul II stood tall in his condemnation of the Iraq war. Nevertheless, the right-wing legacy of the Catholic Church is not easily forgotten.

That the church has always been critical of secularism should come as no surprise. Secularism is, after all, predicated on an understanding of human development without reference to God or some force external to humanity itself.[6] That project took shape during the Enlightenment, and it fundamentally contests the thinking of the faithful. Science explored the internal workings of nature, and human experimentation produced technology. New theories of neoclassical economics and, ultimately, the labor theory of value showed how wealth is generated through human effort, while liberal social contract theory highlighted the rational individual, civil liberties, the right of resistance, and the accountability of public institutions. The only response for traditionalist critics of secularism has been what Ernst Cassirer termed a "mytho-poetic" form of thinking that challenges rationality and the primacy accorded reflection.

Secular liberalism has always threatened the absolute claims of religious institutions and the provincial disposition generated by organic societies with premodern economic arrangements. And religious institutions have always known it. The liberal secular state and liberal secular ideology *together* serve freedom by allowing people to make up their minds on the issues of faith and religious observance. Ratzinger's suggestion that the liberal state should be recognized as a secular institution, even while liberal secularism should be opposed as an ideology, simply dissociates power from legitimacy. It also begs some concrete questions: Should the church act as a controlling mechanism on the liberal state, or should the strictures of the liberal state be privileged in political matters? Has the church ever been willing to regulate itself, without external pressure, even on issues such as the sexual abuse of parishioners? Should rabbinical tribunals decide who is a citizen of Israel? Is it legitimate for an ayatollah to issue a fatwa that contravenes the rule of law? Is the religious belief in democracy real, or is it applicable only when it serves the interests of the church or synagogue or mosque?

Breaking with dogma of any sort is impossible without distinguishing between "faith" and "knowledge." Every attempt to blend reason and faith or offer "fundamental" or "grounding" values through some form of "civic religion"—even when God was placed at the center—has resulted in authoritarian disaster. The point about grounding or foundational values is that they are prepolitical; they remain unconnected with rights or liberties precisely because rights and liberties receive their definition only in political society. The Bible, the Koran, or holy texts from other religions can serve as the source of grounding and prepolitical values. Still, the possible interpretations of these texts are infinite because they all invoke the personal experience of faith. How is one interpretation to be privileged over another, and how are the adherents of the less popular interpretation to be protected?

Other than respect for the basic values underpinning the liberal political order, it seems that the foundational values offered by religion are not quite as self-evident as Ratzinger would like to believe. Women, gays, and those of different beliefs would surely differ with regard to their character, and with all due respect, not everyone agrees that the death of Jesus embodies the "highest expression" of love. The Catholic Church itself caused rivers of blood to flow during the Crusades, the witch burnings, the inquisitions, the pogroms, and endless internecine wars in a host of failed attempts to ascertain what is basic to its own faith. Every interpretation of a holy text has—almost by definition—the possibility of taking on absolute pretensions once the *private* faith informing it is identified with the *public* interests of any religious institution intent on secular power. That is why only the secular democratic state's *respectful indifference* to religious values and the like—what the cardinal terms "reason fallen ill"—can provide the antidote to the "abuse of religion."

The will to know—about stem cell research, about the human genome, about DNA, and about the atom—may not guarantee the ability to use that knowledge properly. But it illuminates how the world and the human being are "made," which need not inevitably lead to destruction. New scientific developments can improve the mental and physical health and the quality of life enjoyed by people everywhere. The same warnings that are now heard with respect to stem cell research and genomes and DNA were also voiced when Galileo, Benjamin Franklin, and Albert Einstein introduced their discoveries. Fearful stalwarts of the old regime have always warned against tampering with "nature" and interfering with the design of God. But what is the alternative? Should some institution like the church arbitrarily prevent that knowledge from coming about?

Democracy has never had anything to fear from reason or experimentation. The most durable democratic societies were created by nations that most self-consciously divided church from state and refused to identify any private belief with the public good. Nations such as Great Britain and the United States developed their democratic traditions in part because of their strong affinity for empiricism, positivism, and pragmatism. Their political arrangements left morality and faith in the province of the individual. That remains the despair of our current pontiff, who wants religion to be more than a kind of "subjective ornament providing a possibly useful kind of motivation." But the fact is that morality and faith *must* be treated this way in a genuinely liberal and democratic political order. That is because it must prize behavior more than belief and insist (following John Locke) that the individual is free to do what the law of the state does not explicitly prohibit. If the pope believes that Enlightenment political thought leads to anarchy, he is seriously mistaken. Postmodernists have been so critical of the Enlightenment legacy precisely because its partisans differentiated clearly between freedom and license. The Enlightenment was ultimately directed against religious fanatics and those who, today, would defend the arbitrary exercise of institutional power. The majority of the philosophes were never concerned with abolishing religion. They were instead concerned with securing the right of each individual not merely to believe or not, in his or her own way, but also to *decide* what is worthy of belief in his or her private existence without having that belief turned into an imperative for the public at large.

What, then, becomes of the common good? Perhaps the multiplication of individual interests, experiences, and opinions is the common good. Or, to put it another way, the common good is the enlargement of freedom and the possibilities for expanding individual experience. *Freedom* is not a word that has much currency in the article written by Cardinal Ratzinger, but it remains decisive: moral reason is an oxymoron if it does not speak to a belief in freedom whose foundational values include respect for the liberal rule of law, an elementary sense of fairness, the accountability of institutions, and the extension of reciprocal rights and obligations equally to all members of the community. Freedom—not some abstract grounding—is the foundation for human self-understanding.

That is essentially what the best of the philosophes sought in political terms. Enlightenment fundamentalism, if there is such a thing, is ultimately predicated not on scientific truth but on privileging individual autonomy and the critical exercise of reason over the claims of unyielding traditions and unaccountable institutions.

Reducing people to things can be undertaken by a variety of institutions and justified by a variety of religions and ideologies. Perhaps a complementary learning process is necessary for the partisans of knowledge as well as the partisans of faith. But if such an encounter were to take place, its goal could only be to break the chains that bind. It would begin by assuming the need for not less freedom but more: more education, more research, more information, more criticism, and more reflection. The real clash is not between civilizations—or what has been termed "the West and the rest"—but between supporters of a secular liberal state with a pluralistic public realm and others intent on imposing their religious convictions on disbelievers.

Faith, myth, and dogma lie at the core of servitude and authoritarianism. Critique, science, and tolerance—by contrast—incarnate what little hope there is for the hopeless. Not religion but reason is on the ropes. The idea that "reason" is somehow *the* problem facing Western societies today is simply to blame the victim. In this world of managed misinformation, communitarian backlash, religious fanaticism, and self-righteous ignorance, it is perhaps useful for all of us—including the pontiff and his followers—to consider the anguished words of his countryman Thomas Mann, which echo from an even darker time: "As if there was ever too much intellect in the world!"

11

False Antinomies

On Religious Conviction and Human Rights

In 2004 I was invited to speak at a conference on human rights in Qom, and this essay—built on that lecture—is a fitting end to *Peace Out of Reach.* It sharply contests Islamic theocracy no less than the signal importance of prepolitical religious values for contemporary democracy. It is also critical of all those provincial nationalists, communitarians, and religious dogmatists who maintain that invoking universal claims always threatens particular experience. I suggest that this is a mistaken way of framing the issue. Exactly the reverse is the case: the degree to which the universal elements underpinning human rights and the liberal rule of law are embraced by the state is the degree to which diverse forms of belief can flourish in civil society. But this means that liberal society must treat faith as a private matter and religious institutions no differently from other interest groups. It follows that such a society must prize behavior more than belief and that it should leave the individual free to do whatever the law does not explicitly prohibit. Imposing such an order by force is another matter. But liberal society with its liberal rule of law inherently contests the arbitrary exercise of power by any institution, even as it tends to expand the possibilities of religious experience. Herein lies the hope it offers to people of faith and the threat it poses to any authoritarian or theocratic order.

As events unfold in the once colonized world in general and the Middle East in particular, it would be a mistake to ignore some of the most pressing philosophical concerns that have been generated in the name of purely strategic issues. The claims forwarded by genuine anti-imperialists and staunch cultural traditionalists that human rights or universalism is a threat to their traditions and customs—and not simply when carried on the point of a bayonet—must be taken seriously. At stake is whether human rights or universalism should be understood positively, as in the general statements formulated by the Vienna Declaration of Human Rights and international bodies such as the United Nations, or whether it should be understood negatively, as the right of each society to embrace the religious customs and historical traditions that make it unique without outside interference.

The first argument is basically political, while the second is primarily cultural. Human rights are correctly associated with the liberal state and its rule of law. They assume equality among citizens, majority rule coupled with protection of the minority, and the ability of the individual to contest time-honored customs and social practices. Human rights have a universal component by definition. That is precisely what allows for a critique of the way the United States—trumpeting its exceptionalism—so often places itself beyond the consensual laws, rules, and agreements of the international community. Insistence on cultural uniqueness, on the contrary, highlights the particular community. Critique and the concerns of the individual are subordinate to the rituals, myths, and symbolic practices of the society. The political stance is formal, while the cultural argument is contextual. The ability to overcome what is generally considered the oppositional nature of these two views depends on confronting the usual ways of framing the debate between the universal and the particular.

Poststructuralists such as Michel Foucault, for example, can suggest that the universal claims made by rationalists and liberals are not only ungrounded and metaphysical but also dangerous, insofar as they repress the particular voice and the singular experience of the outsider. The function of universals thus lies in squashing particularity and diversity. That basic view is shared by most "communitarians." Known for highlighting the role of tradition, myth, and historical experience in building solidarity and binding together a "community," thinkers such as Charles Taylor view universal formulations as empty and culturally imperialistic. As for liberals and rationalists, they have usually been fearful of the experiential, the socially situated, and particular forms of class or national solidarity. The liberal emphasis on legal procedure, civil rights, and an indeterminate understanding of the citizen tends to contest the community in favor of the individual and strip life of its historically transmitted meaning. At best, liberal rationalists admit that universals need not rest on absolute philosophical foundations. Most of them are also willing to compromise with their philosophical foes. The recent work of John Rawls thus argues both for the philosophical primacy of "decency"—a feeling for consensual and respectful forms of conduct beyond any explicitly liberal norms or rules—and for an "overlapping consensus" that stands between the truth claims of particular communities and those of universal charters such as the Vienna Declaration of Human Rights.[1]

Poststructuralists, communitarians, and pragmatists rarely refer to the institutional preconditions for the *free* exercise of particular convictions and beliefs, whereas liberals and rationalists usually do not concern themselves with the element of *resistance* involved in securing the practice of diversity. The debate between these two opposing schools has drained modern philosophy of its political content, its critical character, and its radical sense of purpose.[2] It is therefore necessary to deal with the conflict in a new way that will highlight the moment of action and the exercise of freedom. Or, to put it another way, issues of this sort should not be left to the philosophers.

Meaningful expressions of diversity require institutional and legal mechanisms for universally guaranteeing reciprocity in terms of rights, duties, and the exercise of autonomy. It is here that the practical discussion begins. Many religions consider themselves universal—or "catholic"—in orientation. But the institutional and legal mechanisms they possess for ensuring reciprocity extend, even under the best of circumstances, only to their own flock. In practice, no religious institution is either capable of or (usually) willing to extend reciprocity to those who are not of the faith. Only the federal state—or an international federation of states—under the liberal rule of law can possibly guarantee reciprocity among its citizens and allow for the exercise of particular beliefs. That is because *behavior* with respect to the "other," rather than the presumed superiority of any *conviction*, is the criterion for judgment in a liberal political order.

Liberal notions of law basically rest on what philosophers such as John Stuart Mill refer to as the "harm principle": any activity is legitimate so long as it does no harm to another. Arguments can be made, of course, about the nature of "harm" and whether it can take symbolic form, such as blasphemy. But there is a profound danger in abolishing the distinction between word and deed, for then the distinction between persuasion and coercion vanishes as well. That is an untenable situation. When "harm" is understood purely symbolically—as, for example, an affront to faith—the discourse becomes constrained, and ultimately, a given form of ideological or institutional authority is preserved from criticism. Civil liberties are thereby constricted, and the exercise of freedom is narrowed. The possibilities for exercising diversity thus diminish. Indeed, taking this a step further, it becomes evident that the extent to which authoritarianism exists is the extent to which diversity is denied its citizens.

Providing an "absolute" philosophical foundation for such a claim is probably impossible, but what John Dewey would have called a "warranted assertion" for its legitimacy occurs when one takes even the most cursory look at history. Admittedly, an authoritarian state may offer to protect diversity against even more intolerant domestic foes. Its leaders may also seek to justify themselves by claiming that they are protecting the community from external threats and internal disharmony. But this is an old story.[3] The struggle for liberty has always been the struggle to accord legal recognition to the "outsider": the person without property, the person of another race, the person from another country, the person of another sexual orientation, the person who is incapacitated, the person of another faith.

Universal principles of reciprocity with respect to rights and obligations, no less than the accountability of all institutions, offer a standard for contesting provincial prejudices and positive laws justifying arbitrary government constraints on the various expressions of individuality. Freedom was never the province of a class, a race, a nation, or a religion; it is solely the province of the individual. All movements representing the outsider, whether woman or gay or person of color, have understood that. Their greatest representatives employed liberal values as surely as socialists such as Jean Jaurés or Rosa Luxemburg, who were cognizant that civil liberties serve as the precondition for organizing in the name of economic justice and dealing with the arbitrary power exercised by capital over working people. A socialist understanding of democracy, in this way, builds on the liberal one. Socialist visionaries, along with women, people of color, Catholics, Jews, atheists, and those without property, admittedly had no place in the original framework of liberal thinkers.[4] But this had less to do with some inherent defect of liberalism than with the inability of even its most progressive figures to question their prejudices from the standpoint of their principles.

Although popularizing the notion of a social contract among all citizens did not immediately result in recognizing the legitimacy of every outsider or any particular "other," it ultimately served as the precondition for doing so. Only by ignoring the need for a universal guarantee of reciprocity, or a universal right to engage in dissent and diversity, is it possible to argue that secularism is a form of "deracinated hubris."[5] Contrary to many populist assertions, the secular liberal state was always the hope of the "other," and on the occasions when it wasn't, a "performative contradiction" existed between its principles and its practices. The basic political preoccupation of liberal secularists since the eighteenth century was with rectifying the discrimination suffered by the outsider,[6] who admittedly often became an insider, and with the rational adjudication of grievances over the use of force. As I have written elsewhere, recognizing the dignity of the "other" is the line in the sand marking the great divide between democracy and authoritarianism.

Democracy is usually understood as the will of the majority, but that is a mistake. Authoritarian regimes regularly employ plebiscites, and, given the monopoly of control over what Edward Said called "the forces of knowledge production," there is no reason to suppose that a majority did not support the great totalitarian states of recent memory. Democracy instead rests on the ability to *change* the thinking of the majority, and that is possible only when the security of the minority is established and there is a general commitment not merely to allow but also to encourage individuals to engage in diverse experiences and embrace different ways of dealing with the world. Locke put it well when he wrote in his famous *Second Treatise:* "the end of Law is not to abolish or restrain, but to preserve and enlarge freedom."

Or, to put it another way, the extent to which the liberal rule of law is acting according to its stated purpose is the extent to which diversity can flourish and the individual can choose to identify with what makes him or her particular. Such practices are possible only if individuals can make claims on the public authority; insist on the accountability of all social institutions, including capital; and criticize existing privileges, traditions, and rigid definitions of identity.[7] "Tradition" is no substitute for the liberal rule of law; individuals must often choose between conflicting traditions, and even a single tradition, like a single religion or religious work, is subject to competing interpretations. According to any meaningful understanding of diversity, and any critical understanding of liberalism, the responsibility for his or her fate, whether salvation or damnation, lies with the individual. It resides in the freedom of choice that is the crux of freedom.

Democracy is intended to guarantee the security of the minority, the possibilities of diversity, and the ability of all individuals to expand their range of experiences so long as they do not impede the experiences of others. Tolerance has, for this reason, always been the handmaiden of democracy. The degree of diversity and the freedom of the particular—with respect to individual practices of identity, custom, or religion—depend on the extent to which individual rights are institutionally secured by the liberal state, with its rule of law and universal understanding of the citizen. The imperatives of reciprocity have traditionally been employed in all cultures to contravene the arbitrary exercise of power by "divinely" sanctioned elites, the prejudices they embraced, and the myths they used to justify their positions.

What is crucial about human rights is not their ability to resist unlawful authority or even insist on the equal standing of "outsiders." Rather, it is the new legitimacy human rights provide for such resistance, along with the standpoint of being an outsider. Traditionalists may understand this as nihilism.[8] But in fact, the opposite is the case. Such a stance suggests that freedom is identified less with license than with law and that violent forms of resistance are justified only by situations in which genuine redress for the imposition of arbitrary claims or prejudices is not institutionally available. A progressive understanding of resistance is therefore connected with tolerance, reciprocity, and the exercise of civil liberties.

Customs and religious beliefs often conflict. Securing the right of the individual to judge between traditions or the conflicting interpretations of a single tradition, between religions or the conflicting interpretations of a single religion, has always been the *political* aim of philosophers committed to the Enlightenment legacy. Initially, emphasizing tolerance may have been the only prudent course for dealing with the new pluralism born of markets. But it soon became tied to the indeterminate understanding of the citizen, and this led, ineluctably, to the subjugation of local aristocratic domains to the state and subjugation of the state to the liberal rule of law. Historically, the extent to which this indeterminate understanding of the citizen has been denied is almost always the extent to which the practice of particularity has been constrained and the singular voice has been repressed. Thus, we must rectify a false antinomy: the liberal rule of law with its universal assumptions and its indeterminate notion of the citizen actually serves as the precondition for diversity and the free exercise of the particular.

Traditionalists have always sought to preserve their privileges by insisting that the outsider—whether Jew or Arab, woman or gay, heretic or person of color—is not like other people and is incapable of participating equally in the existing society. The outsider's ability to make a claim against established authority rests not merely on maturity but also (as Kant recognized) on the courage to resist. It is easy enough to turn such courage into a self-serving pose; pornography, the stupidities of MTV, and the like tend to insist on the right to criticize without making clear what purposes such criticism serves. There is something legitimate about what Herbert Marcuse described as "repressive tolerance"—a tolerance servicing the established order—and his demand that it be transformed into a new perspective that privileges the connection between liberty and resistance.[9] Summoning the courage to resist is made easier by liberal institutions and a public that is animated by civic interests. Traditionalism has always inhibited this and the development of what has been termed "individual will formation." Indeed, the more expansive the free play of public opinion, the greater the protection afforded to personal liberty and individual conscience.[10]

The right to be wrong is an element of liberty. What is not an element of liberty, however, is the belief that any given custom or opinion should be perpetuated simply because it has become part of the established wisdom. Civil liberties and the institutional mechanisms for the redress of grievances must be given more than passive legal status. They play a concrete role in fostering the exercise of autonomy. This necessarily results in a perspective whereby the right to criticize turns into a permanent fixture of the liberal rule of law, and the demand for obedience to the established authority becomes a provisional occurrence.[11] Whether to privilege personal liberty over authority is what pits the ideal of Karl Popper's "open society" against the closure of revealed faith. The "outsider," the person concerned with practicing a particular form of identity or belief, benefits from a culture concerned with the former rather than the latter. It is therefore disingenuous to suggest that belief in an open society is just another form of dogma. Such a stance is based on wordplay; it is the same as suggesting that the attack on imperialism is itself imperialistic.

The strengthening of prejudice and intolerance is the underside of the struggle for an expanded understanding of reciprocity and liberty. There is no reason to believe that Jews and Muslims, both of whom suffered persecution under Christianity, should somehow be immune to the forces of reaction. Everywhere a contest is emerging between those who support and those who oppose the double standard. It informs the understanding of Muslims when they insist on being protected from insults and criticisms, even while their texts spew hatred against Jews, Christians, and the Baha'i. The double standard contravenes the liberal rule of law; it undercuts the notion of reciprocity and the possibilities of dialogue; it privileges the self-satisfied beliefs of a community over any sense of cosmopolitan responsibility. Liberalism, social justice, and internationalism all founder on the reef of the double standard. Coming to terms with its exercise is perhaps the central issue for progressives attempting to foster human rights and a genuinely democratic foreign policy.

Not a "clash of civilizations" but rather a clash of two overriding political ideologies is becoming increasingly evident. Cosmopolitan liberal secularism is confronting authoritarian traditionalism in the United States no less than in Saudi Arabia or China. The roots of the conflict are ancient, but when conceived in terms of a new planetary politics,[12] its true ramifications are being felt only now: Israeli refuseniks are stirring against the military occupation in Palestine, Muslim intellectuals are gingerly questioning the validity of Jewish conspiracy theories, and Iranian students are whispering words of rebellion in cafés where only a curtain separates them from men smoking hookahs. Herein lies the basis for a new notion of solidarity, or what I have termed a "cosmopolitan sensibility," which any modern commitment to international democratic institutions and international social justice requires.

From the first, the Enlightenment ethos sought to circumscribe the secular ambitions of all religions. In both the Occident and the Orient, whatever the different social contexts, the battle is still over whether a single religion should dominate public life or whether every religion should be seen as just another private interest with particular political aspirations. Rejecting the latter view is not simply a matter of the church, the synagogue, and the mosque acting in accordance with divine law against the incursions of the profane, although it can be turned into that. Rather, it is a matter of institutional self-preservation. Indeed, for the faithful, the more dramatic the demand for reciprocity, the more fundamental the response will be.

Insisting on a belief in the absolute character of revelatory truth obviously generates a division between the saved and the damned. There arises the simultaneous desire to abolish blasphemy and bring the heathen into the light. Of course, not every person in quest of what the Japanese thinker Nishida termed the "pure experience" is a religious fanatic or obsessed with issues of identity. Making existential sense of reality through the pure experience is a serious matter and a legitimate undertaking. But it follows that the stronger the obsession with determining the purity of the experience, the more fanatical the believer. In progressive political terms, therefore, the problem is not the lack of intensity in the lived life of the individual; it is the attempt by individuals and groups to insist that their own particular and deeply felt existential, religious, or aesthetic experience provides the proper form of intensity.

Religious fundamentalists look backward for their inspiration as surely as integral nationalists and supporters of the organic community do. All of them privilege authority over liberty, unquestioning faith over critical reflection, the revelatory over the demonstrable, and the community over the individual. Each rejects the separation of church from state and the critique of patriarchal hierarchies. Each insists on the legitimacy of traditions simply because they exist. Intolerance and dogmatism are built into this mode of thinking if only because discussion is limited by the holy words of an inerrant Bible or Koran, an infallible pope, the Islamic sharia, or the Jewish halacha. Critique of fundamental assumptions is thereby inhibited from the beginning: fundamentalism ultimately rests on rigid distinctions between the saved and the damned, friend and foe, insider and outsider, the religious ideal and the profane reality. The issue, then, is not really the right of a dominant group to preserve its religious identity from the modern liberal society, but the right of others within that community to practice differently or not at all.

Universal or liberal notions of human rights are important for democracy not only in a heterogeneous community with many religions but also in a homogeneous community with a single religion. After all, it cannot be known in advance what issues and which claims citizens will raise. Just as it is impossible to privilege any particular religion while attempting to be impartial with respect to all, it is impossible to privilege any particular interpretation of a religion while equally respecting the interpretations of others. This is the case because belief inspires practice and because, for the guardians of orthodoxy, it is not simply a matter of being right; it is a matter of being "absolutely" right.

No responsible political person can afford to assume that individuals' shared experience of religiosity will overcome the competing ambitions of diverse religions or that everyone will be tolerant and open-minded simply because they say they will. There is also little historical reason for the outsider to trust the insider, the dissident the establishmentarian, the Jew the Christian, or the black the white. Different communities have different customs and beliefs, but that does not invalidate the importance of making judgments both between and within these diverse communities. It is, again, not a matter of rejecting religion or tradition as such but one of insisting that the individual be able to maximize judgments about which traditions should be kept and which discarded.

Liberty is never a problem for the individual or group that possesses it. The problem arises only when freedom is demanded by the disenfranchised, the exploited, the excluded, the other. Enlightenment political theory thus highlighted the need for reciprocity in the allocation of rights and duties to the state. This creates a strange state of affairs: orthodox Christian, Jewish, or Islamic intellectuals can criticize liberalism, but, according to their fundamentalist beliefs, liberal intellectuals dare not criticize them. With respect to reciprocity, it is the height of arrogance that members of the ultraorthodox communities in Israel are in the forefront of those championing an imperialist policy while simultaneously insisting on their exemption from military duty (the better to pray for victory?). All this is predicated on fundamentalists' refusal to compromise the absolute character of their belief and accept that they should be treated like everyone else.

Conviction and tolerance are no more or less mutually exclusive than the particular and the universal. Dealing politically with any particular belief system is, from the standpoint of democratic principles, actually no different from dealing with any other private interest or ideology. It becomes a matter of securing the institutional conditions for the pursuit of the one and the right to believe in the other. Calling on the faithful to embrace a liberal public sphere is neither blasphemous nor disrespectful. Bringing its principles to bear on issues of belief should result not in a repression of difference but in its liberation and the flowering of conviction.

Notes

2. Lessons from Afghanistan

1. On the exaggerated claims concerning how 9/11 transformed politics and how the Bush administration's reactionary assumptions about foreign policy are grounded in the United States' imperialist history and the "paranoid streak" of American politics, see Stephen Eric Bronner, *Blood in the Sand: Imperial Fantasies, Right-Wing Ambitions, and the Erosion of American Democracy* (Lexington: University Press of Kentucky, 2005), 1–14, 160–84.

2. "The Afghanistan operations to destroy al Qaeda base camps and overthrow the Taliban regime might be justified as strictly defensive responses to 9/11, permitted under the UN Charter, but the excessive cost in human lives there, reaching well over three thousand, raises questions of proportionality." Carl Boggs, *Imperial Delusions: American Militarism and Endless War* (Lanham, MD: Rowman & Littlefield, 2005), 171.

3. Daniel Byman, *Deadly Connections: States That Sponsor Terrorism* (New York: Cambridge University Press, 2005), 215.

4. Michael T. Klare, "Losing the War on Terrorism," www.tomdispatch.com/index.mhtml?pid=47757.

5. Boggs, *Imperial Delusions*, 59.

6. That "reconstruction" is a crucial element of any "just war" is emphasized by Michael Walzer, *Arguing about War* (New Haven, CT: Yale University Press, 2004), 18ff.

7. *Economist*, June 24, 2006.

8. *New York Times*, January 30, 2006.

9. Christian Parenti, "Afghanistan: The Other War," *Nation*, March 27, 2006, 11ff.

10. *Chicago Tribune*, May 17, 2005.

11. The thrust of that conversation is corroborated in an interview conducted by Seymour Hersh with Richard C. Clarke, the former National

Security Council terrorism adviser, who stated that "the Administration viewed Afghanistan as a military and political backwater—a detour along the road to Iraq, the war that mattered most to the president." Seymour M. Hersh, "The Other War," *New Yorker,* www.newyorker.com/printables/fact/040412fa_fact.

12. Reuters, September 29, 2006.

13. www.truthout.org/docs_2006/072306D.shtml.

14. "There is a real possibility that the retaliatory bombing in Afghanistan will turn into the first phase of an all-out conflict with the Islamic world. Under such circumstances, any semblance of a connection between means and ends would be lost." Bronner, *Blood in the Sand,* 24. Also, see Douglas Kellner, "September 11 and the Terror War: The Bush Legacy and the Risks of Unilateralism," in *The* Logos *Reader: Rational Radicalism and the Future of Politics,* ed. Stephen Eric Bronner and Michael J. Thompson (Lexington: University Press of Kentucky, 2006), 303–32.

15. Byman, *Deadly Connections,* 189.

16. "Actually, Al Qaeda, if you look back, was barely mentioned in US intelligence reports until 1998. Clinton's bombing of Sudan and Afghanistan in 1998 effectively created Al Qaeda, both as a known entity in the intelligence world and also in the Muslim world. In fact, the bombings created Osama bin Laden as a major symbol, led to a very sharp increase in recruitment and financing for Al Qaeda–style networks, and tightened relations between bin Laden and the Taliban, which previously had been quite hostile to him." Noam Chomsky, *Imperial Ambitions: Conversations on the Post-9/11 World* (New York: Metropolitan Books, 2005), 108.

17. "For the past 250 years, the ruling group has been the Pushtuns (known also as Pathans), who constitute about 40 percent of the population; Tajiks, 25 percent; Uzbeks, 10 percent; Hazaras, Baluch, and Turkomans, the remainder." Alvin Z. Rubenstein (for the Foreign Policy Institute), "Afghanistan after the Taliban," www.fpri.org/enotes/americawar.20011015.rubenstein.afghanistanaftertaliban.html.

18. Of the 249 members of parliament, there "are forty commanders (warlords) of armed militias, twenty-four members of criminal gangs, seventeen drug traffickers and nineteen men facing serious allegations of war crimes and human rights violations." Ann Jones, "Letter from Afghanistan: Women and Warlords," *Nation,* May 22, 2006, 16, www.tcf.org/list.asp?type=NC&pubid=1176.

19. Hersh, "The Other War," 4.

20. The State Department has acknowledged that Afghanistan is "on the verge of becoming a narcotics state." Roughly 60 percent of its economy, an estimated $2.8 billion, derives from the trafficking of opium, and Afghanistan

accounts for nearly 90 percent of the world's opium production. See Jim Lobe, "Afghanistan: Four Years after US Campaign, Perils Abound," Inter Press Service News Agency, www.ipsnews.net/news.asp?idnews=30545.

21. Zafar Bangash (for Muslimedia), "Two Years after the US Invasion, Afghanis Facing Unprecedented Terror and Abuse," www.muslimedia.com/afg-twoyrs.htm.

22. For an excellent historical and sociological introduction to Afghanistan, see Dilip Hiro, *War without End: The Rise of Terrorism and the Global Response* (London: Routledge, 2002), 179–264.

23. Sheldon Rampton and John Stauber, *Weapons of Mass Deception: The Uses of Propaganda in Bush's War on Iraq* (New York: Tarcher/Penguin, 2003), 175.

24. Noam Chomsky, *Hegemony or Survival: America's Quest for Global Dominance* (New York: Henry Holt, 2003), 162–63.

25. "The term 'blowback,' which officials of the Central Intelligence Agency first invented for their own internal use, is starting to circulate among students of international relations. It refers to the unintended consequences of policies that were kept secret from the American people. . . . Take the civil war in Afghanistan. . . . Over the years the fighting turned Kabul, once a major center of Islamic culture, into a facsimile of Hiroshima after the bomb. American policies helped ensure that the Soviet Union would suffer the same kind of debilitating defeat in Afghanistan as the United States had in Vietnam. In fact, the defeat so destabilized the Soviet regime that at the end of the 1980s it collapsed. But in Afghanistan the United States also helped bring to power the Taliban, a fundamentalist Islamic movement whose policies toward women, education, justice and economic well-being resemble not so much those of Ayatollah Khomeini's Iran as those of Pol Pot's in Cambodia." Chalmers Johnson, *Blowback: The Costs and Consequences of American Empire* (New York: Henry Holt, 2000), 13, 10–11.

26. Officials of the Reagan administration "went beyond supporting them [the mujahideen]. They organized them. They collected radical Islamists from around the world—the most violent, crazed elements they could find—and tried to forge them into a military force in Afghanistan. The mujahideen were armed, trained, and directed by Pakistani intelligence mainly, but under CIA supervision and control, with the support of Britain and other powers. You could argue that this would have been legitimate if it had been for the purpose of defending Afghanistan, but it wasn't. In fact, it probably prolonged the war in Afghanistan. The Soviet archives suggest Moscow was ready to pull out of Afghanistan in the early 1980s. But that wasn't the point. The point was not to defend the Afghans, but to harm the Russians. The mujahideen carried out terrorist activities right inside Russia. And these

same forces later morphed into what became Al Qaeda." Chomsky, *Imperial Ambitions,* 107–8.

27. Consider *Les Miserables* by Victor Hugo, in which a police official obsessively pursues the main character, who stole some bread, for twenty years, or *Caligula,* the play by Albert Camus, in which the madness of the emperor is related to the limitlessness of his desires and his refusal to accept the limits of power.

28. See http://news.yahoo.com/s/nm/20060503/ts_nm/rights_amnesty_dc. See also the fine essay by Lawrence Davidson, "Torture in Our Time," *Logos* 4, no. 4 (Fall 2005), www.logosjournal.com.

29. *New York Times,* February 26, 2006.

30. http://www.truthout.org/docs_2005/121905B.shtml.

3. *The Iraqi Debacle*

1. Stephen Eric Bronner, "Baghdad Memories," in *Blood in the Sand: Imperial Fantasies, Right Wing-Ambitions, and the Erosion of American Democracy* (Lexington: University Press of Kentucky, 2005), 38–48.

2. For a fine critical analysis, see Douglas Kellner, *The Persian Gulf TV War* (Boulder, CO: Westview, 1992).

3. An array of quotations from leading right-wing media celebrities was compiled in "The Final Word Is Hooray! Remembering the Iraq War's Pollyanna Pundits" by Fairness and Accuracy in Media on March 15, 2006, http://www.fair.org/index.php?page=2842. On the decline of the critical liberal, see Tony Judt, "Bush's Useful Idiots," *London Review of Books,* September 21, 2006, and my piece, coauthored with Kurt Jacobsen, "Dub'ya's Fellow Travelers: Left Intellectuals and Mr. Bush's War," in *Blood in the Sand,* 102–18.

4. *Guardian,* October 7, 2005.

5. *New York Times,* December 9, 2005.

6. For a collection of misguided statements on the "victory"—many of which called for "the critics" to apologize—see "The Final Word Is Hooray," www.fair.org/index.php?page=2842.

7. As a commander of coalition forces in Iraq, Peter Chiarelli, put it: "For every one we pick off the streets, we're creating one to take his place." *Economist,* March 25, 2006, 49.

8. *Guardian,* April 27, 2005.

9. Mike Marqusee, "A Name That Lives in Infamy," *Guardian,* November 10, 2005; Peter Popham, "US Forces 'Used Chemical Weapons' during Assault on the City of Fallujah," *Independent,* November 8, 2005.

10. George Monbiot, "Behind the Phosphorus Clouds Are War Crimes within War Crimes," *Guardian,* November 22, 2005.

11. Reuters, October 11, 2006.

12. *Washington Post,* November 12, 2006.

13. http://www.cnn.com/2006/BUSINESS/11/06/corruption.survey.reut/index.html.

14. *New York Times,* August 4, 2006.

15. Two major studies commissioned by the Bush administration stated that Saddam Hussein had already abandoned his nuclear program in 1991 and his chemical weapons program in 1996. See the transcript of David Kay's testimony before the Senate Armed Services Committee, at www.cnn.com/2004/US/01/28/kay.transcript; see also the congressional testimony of Charles Duelfer, director of central intelligence and special adviser for strategy regarding Iraqi weapons of mass destruction, at www.cia.gov/cia/public_affairs/speeches/2004/ tenet_testimony_03302004.html, and his final CIA report at www.msnbc.msn.com/id/7634313.

16. See my article "Anatomy of a Disaster: Class War, Iraq, and the Contours of American Foreign Policy," *Logos* 2, no. 4 (Fall 2003), www.logosjournal.com.

17. *Washington Post,* September 9, 2006.

18. Dexter Filkins, "Where Plan A Left Ahmad Chalabi," *New York Times Magazine,* November 5, 2006, 46.

19. Other memos have been made public, showing that President Bush and Prime Minister Blair were bent on invasion, with or without a UN resolution; were cynical about whether weapons of mass destruction actually existed; and envisioned a quick victory. The president, in fact, predicted that it was "unlikely there would be internecine warfare between the different religious and ethnic groups." *New York Times,* March 27, 2006.

20. See the fine analysis by Mark Danner, *The Secret Way to War: The Downing Street Memo and the Iraq War's Buried History* (New York: NYR Books, 2006).

21. Contrary to early claims about precision bombing and ongoing disclaimers about the use of napalm bombs, according to Colin Brown, writing in the *Independent* (June 17, 2005), it appears that the U.S. military employed MK77 bombs in Iraq. These bombs, based on "an evolution of the napalm used in Vietnam and Korea, carry kerosene-based jet fuel and polystyrene so that, like napalm, the gel sticks to structures and to its victims. The bombs lack stabilizing fins, making them far from precise."

22. http://www.truthout.org/docs_2005/061606L.shtml.

23. *Guardian,* June 23, 2005.

24. *New York Times,* September 24, 2006.

25. The veracity of the Downing Street memo was confirmed through the research of the subcommittee led by Representative John Conyers. See http://www.uruknet.info/?p=19112&hd=0&size=1&1 =x.

26. See *Guardian*, February 24, 2006, http://technology.guardian.co.uk/news/story/0,,1716842,00.html.

27. Peter Galbraith, "Last Chance for Iraq," *New York Review of Books*, October 6, 2005, 20.

28. *Washington Post*, August 21, 2005.

29. *New York Times*, September 29, 2006.

30. *Washington Post*, August 14, 2005.

4. *Twilight in Tehran*

1. In a virtual replay of the days leading up to the invasion of Iraq, Bush administration supporters in the House of Representatives published a report exaggerating the speed of Iran's nuclear program. It was immediately attacked by the United Nations' International Atomic Energy Agency for making "erroneous, misleading and unsubstantiated statements." *Washington Post*, September 14, 2006.

2. Among these intellectuals was the leading Iranian philosopher Ramin Jahanbegloo, who was interviewed in *Logos* 5, no. 2 (Spring–Summer 2006), www.logosjournal.com.

3. All the major factions of the United Iraq Alliance—the Supreme Council for the Islamic Revolution, the Dawa, and the forces led by Moktada al-Sadr—along with their paramilitary organizations, are openly sponsored by Iran. "Democracy in Iraq [thus] brought to power Iran's allies who are in a position to ignite an uprising against American troops that would make the current problems with the Sunni insurgency seem insignificant. Iran, in effect, holds the US hostage in Iraq, and as a consequence we have no good military or non-military options in dealing with the problem of Iran's nuclear facilities. Unlike the 1979 hostage crisis, we did this to ourselves." Peter Galbraith, "The Mess," *New York Review of Books*, March 9, 2006, 27.

4. "With each American military strike in the region, first against the Taliban in Afghanistan and then against Saddam Hussein in Iraq, Iran has found its influence in the region grow as its enemies have been defeated by American military might." *New York Times*, March 13, 2006.

5. A fine study of this seminal action on the part of the United States can be found in Stephen Kinzer, *All the Shah's Men: An American Coup and the Roots of Middle East Terror* (New York: John Wiley, 2003).

6. In 2003 the Iranian government "was prepared to make concessions

about its nuclear program and to address concerns about its ties to groups such as Hezbollah and Islamic Jihad, in return for an agreement from the White House to refrain from destabilizing the Islamic republic and start lifting long-in-effect sanctions. The U.S. rejected the overture out of hand. It seemed that Bush didn't want to offer guarantees to a regime that he intended, at a later date, to try to destroy." Christopher de Bellaigue, "Defiant Iran," *New York Review of Books,* November 2, 2006, 58.

7. Ali Gheissari and Vali Nasr, *Democracy in Iran: History and the Quest for Liberty* (New York: Oxford University Press, 2006).

8. Hooshang Amirahmadi, "In the Name of the Iranian People: Regime Change or Regime Reform?" *Logos* 5, no. 2 (Spring–Summer 2006), www.logosjournal.com.

9. One specialist on Iran has noted that "the United States is preparing a sustained bombing campaign in Iran in hopes of halting the country's nuclear program, coupled with revelations that the Pentagon has been using an Iranian terrorist organization called the Mujahedin-e Khalq (MEK) to conduct stealth operations in Iran from bases in Iraq and Pakistan. [This has] pushed the already paranoid clerical regime into a panic. As happened during the Iran-Iraq war, the regime has begun clamping down even harder on dissent so that activists [such as Nobel Prize winner Shirin] Ebadi who seek a compromise on the nuclear impasse and détente with the West are increasingly being denounced as US stooges." Reza Aslan, "Woman Warrior," *Nation,* May 29, 2006.

10. *New York Times,* August 25, 2005.

11. *New York Times,* August 3, 2005, and April 13, 2006.

12. www.globalresearch.ca/CH0505A.html.

13. Mark LeVine, *Why They Don't Hate Us: Lifting the Veil on the Axis of Evil* (Oxford: Oneworld Publications, 2005).

14. *International Herald Tribune,* November 21, 2005.

15. See Milbry Polk and Angela M. H. Schuster, eds. *The Looting of the Iraq Museum, Baghdad: The Lost Legacy of Ancient Mesopotamia* (New York: Harry Abrams, 2005).

16. See Robin Wright, *The Last Great Revolution: Turmoil and Transformation in Iran* (New York: Vintage, 2001).

17. A joke was making the rounds during the week I spent in Tehran just after the election. It goes like this: A man marries a woman who was married before, but he finds out that she is still a virgin. He asks her how that is possible, and she replies that her first husband was like Khatami: he promised a lot but never delivered.

18. See http://www.iran-press-service.com/ips/articles-2005/November-2005/culturecrackdown261105.shtml.

19. Hadi Ghaemi, "For Iran, the Man Is the Message," *New York Times,* June 29, 2006, A25.

20. A different perspective, which envisions the United States prepared "to set Israel loose" to attack Iran, is argued by Michel Chossudovsky (for the Centre for Research on Globalization), "Planned US-Israeli Attack on Iran," www.globalresearch.ca/articles/CH0505A.html.

21. Seymour Hersh, "Last Stand," *New Yorker,* July 10, 2006.

22. *Guardian,* October 19, 2005.

23. *Washington Post,* April 2, 2006.

24. Conn Hallinan, "Targeting Tehran," *Foreign Policy in Focus,* www.fpif.org.

25. http://news.yahoo.com/s/nm/20060305/ts_nm/nuclear_iran_usa_dc.

26. *New York Times,* November 8, 2005.

27. See "US and Iran: Is Washington Planning a Military Strike?" *Der Spiegel,* December 31, 2005, www.truthout.org/docs_2005/010106Y.shtml.

28. Dariush Zahedi and Omid Memarian, "Ahmadinejad, Iran, and America," *openDemocracy,* February 1, 2007, http://www.opendemocracy.net/democracy-irandemocracy/election_ahmadinejad_4248.jsp.

5. Syria and Its President

1. It is important to consider that Syria, like Iraq, Lebanon, and Kuwait, 0was the product of a disintegrating Ottoman Empire and has been subject to the various imperialist ambitions of England, France, and later the United States. For an excellent study of the Ottoman Empire in its last phase, see David Fromkin, *A Peace to End All Peace: The Fall of the Ottoman Empire and the Creation of the Modern Middle East* (New York: Henry Holt, 1989).

2. *New York Times,* April 5, 2006.

3. *Economist,* October 29, 2005.

4. *Washington Post,* October 25, 2005.

5. Consider the lifting of alien and sedition laws during the War of 1812, the suspension of habeas corpus during the Civil War, the strengthening of censorship and the anticommunist Palmer raids in the years surrounding World War I, the internment of Japanese citizens during World War II, the rise of McCarthyism with the onset of the cold war, and the illegal activities of the FBI during the heyday of the civil rights movement and the Vietnam War. For more on this, see Alan Wolfe, *The Seamy Side of Democracy,* 2nd ed. (Boston: Longman, 1978), and Robert Justin Goldstein, *Political Repression in Modern America: From 1873 to 1976* (Chicago: University of Illinois Press, 2001).

6. John Yoo, *The Powers of War and Peace: The Constitution and Foreign Affairs after 9/11* (Chicago: University of Chicago Press, 2005); Peter Berkowitz, ed., *Terrorism, the Laws of War, and the Constitution: Debating the Enemy Combatant Cases* (Stanford, CA: Hoover Institution Press, 2005).

7. Reza Aslan, *No God but God: The Origins, Evolution, and the Future of Islam* (New York: Random House, 2005); Khaled Abou el Fadl, *Islam and the Challenge of Democracy,* ed. Joshua Cohen and Deborah Chasman (Princeton, NJ: Princeton University Press, 2004).

8. Note the discussions in Cohen and Chasman, *Islam and the Challenge of Democracy.*

9. *New York Times,* October 21, 2005.

10. *New York Times,* December 7, 2005.

11. *New York Times,* June 11, 2006.

12. *New York Times,* December 13, 2005.

13. *New York Times,* October 15, 2005.

14. www.time.com/time/world/article/0,8599,1214903,00.html?cnn+yes.

15. Seymour M. Hersh, "Up in the Air: Where Is the Iraq War Headed Next?" *New Yorker,* November 5, 2005.

16. *New York Times,* September 17, 2005.

17. *New York Times,* July 22, 2006.

18. http://news.yahoo.com/s/ap/20060723/ap_on_re_mi_ea/lebanon israel.

6. *Withdrawal Pains*

1. Precision-guided missiles were rushed to Israel by the Bush administration as part of a multimillion-dollar arms package. Israel had requested the expedited shipment in the wake of its assault on Hezbollah in Lebanon. *New York Times,* July 21, 2006.

2. A more radical view is taken by John J. Mearsheimer and Stephen M. Walt, "The Israel Lobby and US Foreign Policy," *London Review of Books,* March 23, 2006. For comments about this article, see Michael Massing, "The Storm over the Israel Lobby," *New York Review of Books,* June 8, 2006, and Kurt Jacobsen, "The Great 'Israel Lobby' Fuss," *Logos* (Summer 2006), www.logosjournal.com. The American Task Force on Palestine has also compiled a reading list on the controversy; see http://americantaskforce.org/israellobby.htm.

3. The basic problem lies not in the withdrawal from the Occupied Territories but in the Jewish settlements that would supposedly remain and the fact that the West Bank and Gaza would be like islands in an Israeli sea.

An editorial in the *New York Times* (May 26, 2006) made the situation very clear: "To get an idea of this, imagine a map of Manhattan. The West Bank would be, very roughly, East Harlem and the Upper East Side. Gaza would be Battery Park City, far to the southwest. Now imagine trying to create a fully functioning city with its own economy out of those pieces while an entirely independent antagonistic city remained in between." Further, "If Mr. Olmert moves forward with his plan to retain large settlement blocs in the West Bank, the Palestinians may well lose huge parts of their 'Upper East Side' and be left trying to form a country out of what's left and their 'Battery Park City.'"

4. The right to a hot pursuit for purposes of "self-defense," the need to strike Syrian military targets in Lebanon and "select targets in Syria proper," and the desire to use a "firm" hand to deal with the Palestinian Authority were concerns raised in 2000 in "A Clear Break: A New Strategy for Security in the Realm," prepared by a study group composed of prominent neoconservatives such as Richard Perle, Douglas Feith, and others under the auspices of the Institute for Advanced Strategic and Political Studies in Jerusalem; see www.iasps.org/strat1.htm.

5. "To suggest Hizbullah attacked on the orders of Tehran and Damascus is to grossly oversimplify a strong strategic and ideological relationship. . . . Since Syrian forces left Lebanon, Hizbullah has become the stronger party. It has never allowed any foreign power to dictate its military strategy." Amal Saad-Ghorayeb, "The Framing of Hizbullah," www.guardian.co.uk/Israel/comment/0,,1821036,00.html (accessed July 15, 2006).

6. See "History of Israeli-Arab Prisoner Exchanges," Palestine Center Information Brief No. 141 (July 13, 2006).

7. "Hezbollah remains the only military force that the Israelis really respect, based on its top-notch training and equipment supplied by Iran, and a brand of Shiite Islam that lends both extreme discipline and total fearlessness." Mitchell Prothero, "Lebanon Pays for Hezbollah's Sins," www.salon.com/news/feature/2006/07/14/lebanon/.

8. *Gush Shalom,* March 26, 2005.

9. See Gideon Levy, "They Broke the Public's Heart," http://www.haaretz.com/hasen/spages/595104.html.

10. Given the enormous amount of financial and military aid provided by the United States to Israel, the relationship between the two countries actually mirrors that between Iran-Syria and Hezbollah. The events of 2006 were as follows: "earlier this summer, before the Hezbollah kidnappings, the U.S. government consultant said, several Israeli officials visited Washington, separately, 'to get a green light for the bombing operation and to find out how much the United States would bear.' The consultant adds, 'Israel began

with Cheney. It wanted to be sure that it had his support and the support of his office and the Middle East Desk of the Security Council.' After that, 'persuading Bush was never a problem, and Condi Rice was on board,' the consultant said." Seymour M. Hersh, "Watching Lebanon," *New Yorker,* August 21, 2006, www.truthout.org/docs_2006/081306Y.shtml.

11. For an interesting perspective on the history of the Jewish settlements—one that sees them as the product of a policy committed to neither annexation nor return of the territories vanquished in the 1967 war—see Gershom Gorenberg, *The Accidental Empire: Israel and the Birth of the Settlements, 1967–1977* (New York: Times Books, 2006).

12. Lowenstein, "The Disengaged," 4.

13. Menachem Klein, "Jerusalem without East Jerusalemites: The Palestinian as the 'Other' in Jerusalem," *Journal of Israeli History* 23, no. 2 (Autumn 2004): 190.

14. *New York Times,* April 12, 2004.

15. The Applied Research Institute of Jerusalem, whose director is Jad Issac, provides the most instructive maps. See http://www.poica.org/proj-objectives/proj_obj.php.

16. More than 90 percent of Israeli Jews agree that the state should maintain its Jewish majority, more than 80 percent believe that decisions concerning the character of the state should be made by the Jewish majority, and 33 percent of Jewish citizens believe that Palestinian citizens should be granted equal rights. Also, just about one-third of Jewish citizens support the idea of "transferring" Palestinian citizens from Israel. This information is summarized in Yoav Peled, "Zionist Realities," *New Left Review* 38 (March–April 2006): 31.

17. Uri Davis, Ilan Pappe, and Tamar Yaron, "What May Come after the Evacuation of Jewish Settlers from the Gaza Strip," *Counterpunch,* July 15, 2005.

18. See the maps included in "States of Despair: History, Politics, and the Struggle for Palestine," in Stephen Eric Bronner, *Blood in the Sand: Imperial Fantasies, Right-Wing Ambitions, and the Erosion of American Democracy* (Lexington: University Press of Kentucky, 2005), 60–81.

19. The vote for Hamas "was an expression of deeply felt, if unarticulated, anger at years of lost dignity and self-respect, coupled with a yearning to recover a semblance of both. As many Palestinians saw it, they had been on the receiving end of constant demands while Israel still occupied their land with impunity. For years, the Palestinian Authority stood by helplessly during Israeli military incursions. It was asked to defend Israelis from Palestinian attacks, but prohibited from doing the reverse. . . . Because of all it did, said, and stood for, a vote for Hamas became one way to exorcise the disgrace."

Hussein Agha and Robert Malley, "Hamas: The Perils of Power," *New York Review of Books,* March 9, 2006, 22.

20. *New York Times,* April 8, 2006.

21. Marjorie Cohn, "Israel's Gaza Problem," *Alternet,* July 4, 2006, www.alternet.org/story/38488; Virginia Tilley, "Starving in the Dark," *Counterpunch,* June 30, 2006, www.counterpunch.org/ tilley06302006.html.

22. *New York Times,* August 12, 2006.

23. Henry M. Pachter, "Defining an Event: Prolegomenon to Any Future Philosophy of History," *Social Research* 41, no. 3 (Autumn 1974).

24. Lawrence Davidson, "Blitzkrieg Gaza—2006," *Logos* (Spring–Summer 2006), www.logosjournal.com.

25. The "Prisoner's Manifesto" is reprinted in the Spring 2006 issue of *Logos,* www.logosjournal.com.

7. The Middle East Spills Over

1. See "Sudan: International Religious Freedom Report," released by the Bureau of Democracy, Human Rights, and Labor on September 15, 2006.

2. Associated Press, September 17, 2006.

3. *Washington Post,* September 5, 2006.

4. More credence was given to anti-Western voices when it became public that the Joint Chiefs of Staff had been pressing for many months for the creation of an American military command focused solely on Africa. Reuters, September 23, 2006.

5. George Packer, "Letter from Sudan," *New Yorker,* September 11, 2006.

6. IRIN, September 14, 2006.

7. Khartoum's most important representative on Darfur, Majzou al-Khalifa, is quoted as saying: "There is a third way. . . . Why not let the UN place its men, command expertise and material at the service of the African Union mission?" Associated Press, September 26, 2006.

8. See IRIN, September 14, 2006.

9. *Genocide* is not merely a general term but an official designation that, according to the 1948 Convention on the Prevention of Genocide, requires action to halt it. Controversy therefore surrounds the definition of what is occurring in Darfur. Jonathan Steele addressed the matter in a particularly blunt fashion in the *South Africa Press* (September 19, 2006): "In spite of efforts to describe the killing in Darfur as genocide, neither the UN nor the EU went along with this description [due to] the difference between a brutal civil war and a deliberate policy of ethnic cleansing. Darfur is not Rwanda.

Only the U.S. accepted the genocide description, though this seemed a concession to domestic lobbies rather than a matter of conviction. Washington never followed through with the forcible intervention in Darfur that international law requires once a finding of genocide is made." http://r02.webmail.aol.com/19939/aol/en-us/mail/display-message.aspx.

10. Associated Press, September 15, 2006.

11. In 2005 "the UN Security Council passed a historic resolution calling for the Prosecutor of the International Criminal Court (ICC) to investigate war crimes in Darfur. The ICC will help establish a public record, deter future crimes, promote victim reparation, help catalyze reform in Sudan's courts, and assign individual—not group—responsibility for the crimes. These are critical components to reconciliation." *Amnesty International* (Fall 2006): 15.

12. *Washington Post*, September 14, 2006.

13. With regard to UN Resolution 1706, which concerned the deployment of troops to the Sudan, Kristen Silverberg, the assistant secretary of state for international organization affairs, said on September 15, 2006, that "it's absolutely the case" that a military force could be dispatched without the consent of the Sudanese government, and the United States insisted that "there be no language in the resolution that required explicit endorsement of the Sudanese government." "On-the-Record Briefing on the Upcoming United Nations General Assembly."

14. Jeffrey D. Sachs, *The End of Poverty: Economic Possibilities for Our Time* (New York: Penguin, 2005), 5–74, 226–66.

8. Conspiracy Then and Now

1. For a more thorough analysis, see Stephen Eric Bronner, *A Rumor about the Jews: Anti-Semitism, Conspiracy, and the Protocols of Zion* (New York: Oxford University Press, 2000).

2. On the dynamic between centralizing forms of group identity, which strengthen existential feelings of superiority, and the "differentiating" impact of groups that seemingly threaten those feelings, see the now forgotten work by Arnold Zweig, *Caliban oder Politik und Leidenschaft Versuch ueber die menschlichen Gruppenleidenschaften dargetan am Antisemitismus* (1927; reprint, Berlin: Aufbau, 1993).

3. The Continental empires all witnessed the political retreat of the bourgeoisie during the nineteenth century and the transformation of liberalism into the ideology of an economic elite. The mass base for the republican vision was, instead, the proletariat that was inspired by "orthodox Marxism"

and organized in the huge social democratic parties of what was known as the Second International. It is interesting that the labor movement found its recruits in nations that were nondemocratic and that it had problems finding support in nations that already had a republican system. See John H. Kautsky, *Social Democracy and the Aristocracy: Why Socialist Labor Movements Developed in Some Industrial Countries and Not in Others* (New Brunswick, NJ: Transaction, 2002).

4. The Nazis merely substituted *Aryan* for *Christian* in the ongoing historical battle with the Jews. See Adolf Hitler, *Mein Kampf*, trans. Ralph Mannheim (Boston: Houghton Mifflin, 1943), 300, passim.

5. To be sure, the situation was more complicated in what remained of the Ottoman Empire, where an indigenous bourgeoisie and a proletariat were lacking. But various "Young Turks" were rabidly anti-Semitic, and in turn, important British policy makers believed that they were part of a conspiracy led by the Jews and buttressed by Germany that brought down the czar and led to the Bolshevik regime. See the classic study by David Fromkin, *A Peace to End All Peace: The Fall of the Ottoman Empire and the Creation of the Modern Middle East* (New York: Henry Holt, 1989), 245ff, 480, passim.

6. Ernst Piper, *Alfred Rosenberg: Hitler's Chefideologe* (Munich: Karl Blessing Verlag, 2006).

7. See the insightful essay by George L. Mosse, "Community in the Thought of Nationalism, Fascism, and the Radical Right," in *Confronting the Nation: Jewish and Western Nationalism* (Hanover, NH: University Press of New England, 1993), 41ff.

8. Cf. Norman Cohn, *Warrant for Genocide: The Myth of the Jewish World-Conspiracy and the Protocols of the Elders of Zion* (London: Eyre & Spottiswoode, 1967).

9. Carl Boggs, *Imperial Delusions: American Militarism and Endless War* (Lanham, MD: Rowman & Littlefield, 2005), 186.

10. On the American view of Israel, see Lawrence Davidson, *America's Palestine: Popular and Official Perceptions from Balfour to Israeli Statehood* (Gainesville: University Press of Florida, 2001).

11. Bronner, *A Rumor about the Jews*, 129ff.

12. Edward W. Said, *The Politics of Dispossession: The Struggle for Palestinian Self-Determination, 1969–1994* (New York: Vintage, 1995), 247ff.

13. It is interesting that there is very little disagreement over the facts of the Arab expulsion (or *nachbar*) by the two most famous Israeli "revisionist" historians, even though they have radically different political beliefs. Cf. Ilan Pappe, *A History of Modern Palestine: One Land, Two Peoples* (Cambridge: Cambridge University Press, 2003), and Benny Morris, *The Birth of the*

Palestinian Refugee Problem Revisited (Cambridge: Cambridge University Press, 2003).

14. For a more elaborate argument, see Stephen Eric Bronner, "Making Sense of Hell: Three Meditations on the Holocaust," *Political Studies* 47, no. 2 (June 1999): 314–28.

15. Greg Palast, "Was the Invasion of Iraq a Jewish Conspiracy?" *Tikkun* (July–August 2006).

16. A pro-Israeli report that claimed that 40 percent of all Swedes are anti-Semitic defined an anti-Semite as anyone who was critical of Israeli policies. It turns out that actual anti-Semitism among the Swedes is negligible. Meanwhile, "68% of Israeli Jews would refuse to live in the same building as an Arab Israeli, and 40% think that the Israeli government should encourage them to leave the country." See the article by Kristoffer Larsson in *Counterpunch,* http://www.counterpunch.org/larrson04152006.html.

9. *Incendiary Images*

1. I had the honor of writing the afterword to this wonderful work by Will Eisner, *The Plot: The Secret Story of the Protocols of the Elders of Zion* (New York: W. W. Norton, 2005).

2. Stephen Eric Bronner, *A Rumor about the Jews: Anti-Semitism, Conspiracy, and the Protocols of Zion* (New York: Oxford University Press, 2000).

3. *New York Times,* February 12, 2006.

4. James J. Zogby, "Press Misses Point in Cartoon Controversy," www.truthout.org/docs_2006/ 021406F.shtml.

5. Sayeed Hasan Khan and Kurt Jacobsen, "Experiencing Islam, British Style," *Economic and Political Weekly,* February 4, 2006.

6. A Pew poll shows that among non-Muslim Europeans, overall attitudes toward Muslims have generally improved; the same is true for Muslims dealing with non-Muslim Europeans. European Muslims apparently approve of women entering the public sphere, support a moderate version of their religion, and basically do not view Europeans as hostile. The two groups differ most strongly on foreign affairs, with the majority of European Muslims opposing the American "war on terror." By country, 83 percent of Muslims in Spain oppose the "war on terror," as do 79 percent in France, 77 percent in Britain, and 62 percent in Germany. *New York Times,* July 8, 2006.

7. *Economist,* February 11, 2006, 25.

8. At Zundel's trial, surely "observers are hoping for a mention of his

pet theory that the Nazis invented UFOs, and still fly them from a base in Antarctica." *Economist,* February 25, 2006, 57.

9. Ronald Dworkin, "Even Bigots and Holocaust Deniers Must Have Their Say," comment@guardian.co.uk 2/14/06.

10. Of Reason and Faith

1. At the University of Regensburg, on the fourth day of a six-day tour of his native Bavaria, the pope quoted Byzantine Emperor Manuel II in conversation with "an educated Persian": "Show me just what Muhammad brought that was new, and there you will find things only evil and inhuman, such as his command to spread by the sword the faith he preached." Tracy Wilkenson, "Pope, Citing Islam, Criticizes Holy Wars and Fanaticism," *Los Angeles Times,* September 13, 2006.

2. This article has a history. It essentially summarizes the position taken by the pontiff in his debate with the preeminent philosopher Jürgen Habermas, which took place before a small invited audience on January 1, 2004, at the Catholic Academy in Munich. Cardinal Ratzinger argued the importance of "prepolitical" foundations for a liberal secular state and a universal notion of common law derived from "nature"—although what the former actually implies and what the latter can concretely contribute to the liberal state remains unclear. As for Habermas, when accepting the Peace Prize of the *Deutschen Buchhandels* in October 2001, his speech emphasized the need to reconnect "faith" *(Glauben)* and "knowledge" *(Wissen)* and "translate" the "religious content" of moral concepts into a "secular language." For him, it was a matter of salvaging the "original religious meaning" of existence that modernity was eroding or ignoring. Thus, in spite of his belief that reason must still control religious faith, his position ultimately reflects the shift from a "postmetaphysical" to a "postsecular" theory. For more on this, see http://theodor-frey.de/dialog.htm; http://religion.orf.at/projekt02/news/0401/ne040120_harbermas_ratzinger.htm; http://www.sbg.ac.at/sot/texte/2004–01–22-zsf-merkur.htm; and, in English, http://marston.blogspot.com/ 2005/05/habermas-ratzinger.html.

3. Stephen Eric Bronner, *Reclaiming the Enlightenment: Toward a Politics of Radical Engagement* (New York: Columbia University Press, 2004).

4. Norberto Bobbio, *Ideological Profile of Twentieth-Century Italy,* trans. Lydia G. Cochrane (Princeton, NJ: Princeton University Press, 1995).

5. See the reprint of the anthology *The God That Failed,* ed. Richard Crossman (New York: Columbia University Press, 2001).

6. Understanding the "constitution" of reality without reference to God or some force external to humanity is a basic theme not of traditional forms of materialism, such as empiricism or positivism, but rather of philosophical idealism. See Stephen Eric Bronner, "Sketching the Lineage: The Critical Method and the Idealist Tradition," in *Of Critical Theory and Its Theorists*, 2nd ed. (New York: Routledge, 2002), 11ff.

11. False Antinomies

1. John Rawls, *Political Liberalism* (New York: Columbia University Press, 1995); John Rawls, *The Law of Peoples* (Cambridge, MA: Harvard University Press, 2001).

2. Stephen Eric Bronner, *Ideas in Action: Political Tradition in the Twentieth Century* (Lanham, MD: Rowman & Littlefield, 1999), 17–54.

3. That has traditionally served as the justification for *raison d'état*. For a more complete analysis, see Friedrich Meinecke, *Machiavellism: The Doctrine of* Raison d'État *and Its Place in Modern History* (New Brunswick, NJ: Transaction, 1997).

4. Cf. Carol Pateman, *The Sexual Contract* (Stanford, CA: Stanford University Press, 1988); Charles Mills, *The Racial Contract* (Ithaca, NY: Cornell University Press, 1989).

5. Such is the position of Ashis Nandy, *Bonfire of Creeds* (New York: Oxford University Press, 2004). For an opposing view, see Meera Nanda, *Prophets Facing Backward: Postmodern Critiques of Science and Hindu Nationalism in India* (New Brunswick, NJ: Rutgers University Press, 2003).

6. Stephen Eric Bronner, *Reclaiming the Enlightenment: Toward a Politics of Radical Engagement* (New York: Columbia University Press, 2004), 41–60.

7. Note the discussion on how identity is narrowed in the interests of hegemonic groups and institutions by Amartya Sen, *Identity and Violence: The Illusion of Destiny* (New York: W. W. Norton, 2006).

8. Leo Strauss, *Natural Right and Human History* (Chicago: University of Chicago Press, 1965).

9. Herbert Marcuse, "Repressive Tolerance," in *A Critique of Pure Tolerance* (Boston: Beacon, 1969), 81ff.

10. Jurgen Habermas, "The Public Sphere: An Encyclopedia Article," in *Critical Theory and Society: A Reader*, ed. Stephen Eric Bronner and Douglas Kellner (New York: Routledge, 1989), 136ff.

11. Alfred Cobban, *In Seach of Humanity: The Role of the Enlightenment in Modern History* (New York: George Braziller, 1960), 94.

12. Stephen Eric Bronner, ed., *Planetary Politics: Human Rights, Terror, and Global Society* (Lanham, MD: Rowman & Littlefield, 2005).

Index

Abbas, Mahmoud, 85, 86
ABC, 20
Abd Al-Rahman Mohammed, Ahmed, 96, 97–98
Abizaid, John, 28
Abu Ghraib torture scandal, 7, 61
Abu Laban (Danish imam), 128
Abu Shouck (Darfur IDP camp), 96
accountability, 6–7, 151, 153
Action Française, 114
Adorno, Theodor W., 123
Afghanistan: blowback in, 21, 163–64nn25–26; Bush administration cost-shifting in, 22; cartoon protests in, 128–29; civil war in, 18, 163n25; Clinton administration bombing of (1998), 162n16; democratic preconditions absent in, 19, 21; drug trafficking in, 162–63n20; elections (2005), 18; ethnic loyalties in parliament of, 18–19; as failed state, 16–17, 162n18, 162–63n20; guerilla movements in, 21; Iraqi insurgency as model for, 19; NATO troops in, 17; parliament of, 162n18; post-invasion economy, 15–16, 17–18; as potential quagmire, 22; prisoner torture in, 22–23; Soviet occupation of (1979–89), 17–18, 21, 163n25; Taliban integration needed in, 21–22; Taliban resurgence in, 1, 16–17, 18, 21–22; tribalism in, 18–19, 162n17; U.S. foreign policy failure in, 1, 20–21; U.S. military bases in, 20, 45, 52. *See also* Taliban
Afghanistan, U.S. invasion of: 9/11 attacks and, 13–14, 161n2; casualties in, 14; culpability in, 14–15; as disproportionate response, 161n2; impact on al Qaeda, 14; implications of, 162n14; Iranian influence and, 166n4; Iraq invasion as distraction from, 16, 161–62n11; reconstruction efforts following, 15–16; Sudanese anti-Western sentiments and, 95
African Union: Darfur relief efforts and, 103; Khartoum government flexibility on, 98; regional conferences sponsored by, 103–4; regional interest represented by, 100–101; UN "rehatting" of troops of, 94, 101, 172n7
Agha, Hussein, 171–72n19
Ahmadinejad, Mahmoud: anti-

Semitic statements of, 53, 110–11, 128; authoritarian measures of, 50; domestic resistance to, 50–51, 56; elected Iranian president, 42; election campaign issues, 52; nuclear issue embraced by, 52–53, 56
Akkab (Palestine), 83
Al Akysa brigade, 89
Alexander the Great, 49
Algeria, 62, 67
Alwan, Felah, 34
American Enterprise Institute, 55
American Israeli Public Affairs Committee (AIPAC), 55
Anata (Palestine), 83
ancien régime, collapse of, 111–12
Annan, Kofi, 98, 106
anticommunism, 168n5
anti-Semitism: chameleon effect and genocide, 115–16; criticism of Israeli policy vs., 110–11, 117–21; as explanatory device, 111–13, 174n5; in Iran, 44, 46, 53–54; irrational justifications for, 110, 114–15; Islamic fanaticism and, 130–31; Israeli assaults on Lebanon/Gaza and, 77; Israeli double standards and, 175n16; in political cartoons, 125; rebirth of, and U.S. foreign policy failure, 1, 9; social acceptability of, in interwar Europe, 113–15; theory vs. practical implications, 116–17. *See also* "Protocols of the Elders of Zion, The"
Arab League, 98
Arafat, Yasir, 67, 84, 89
Arendt, Hannah, 22, 116
Ariana Hotel (Kabul), 23
Assad, Bashar al-: educational background of, 60; Hariri assassination and, 66–68; as modernizer, 64; peace initiatives of, 71–72; self-serving behavior of, 61–62, 63–64; U.S.-Syrian relations and, 70–72; U.S. visas denied to, 71
Assad, Hafez al-, 59
Atlantic Charter, 137
Austria, 130
Austro-Hungarian Empire, collapse of, 111
authoritarianism: external pressure and, in Iran, 45–46, 50–51, 53–54; liberal secularism vs., 156–57; plebiscites in, 152; provincialism and, 4; religious faith and, 142, 145; Syrian legacy of, 59; "us vs. them" mentality and, 3
Avinery, Uri, 77
"axis of evil," 44

Baath Party: Iraqi, 26, 28; Syrian, 59, 60
Badr Organization, 36
Baghdad (Iraq), 27
Bagram (Afghanistan), military detention facility in, 23
Baker, James, 38, 70
Bangladesh, 64, 128
Barghouti, Murwan, 90
Bashir, Omar Hassan Al-, 94, 95, 98–99
Bechtel, 33
Beit Hanoun (Palestine), 82
Benedict XVI, Pope. *See* Ratzinger, Josef

Benjamin, Jessica, 75
bin Laden, Osama, 13–14, 15, 21, 162n16. *See also* al Qaeda
Blair, Tony, 31, 165n15
blasphemy, 126, 130, 150, 157
Blix, Hans, 31
Bloomberg School of Public Health, 27
blowback, 21, 163–64nn25–26
Boggs, Carl, 161n2
Bolsheviks, 174n5
Bolton, John, 26, 30, 55, 68
bourgeoisie, 9, 11, 111–12, 173–74n3
Brammertz, Serge, 68
Bronner, Stephen Eric, 177n6
Brown, Colin, 165n21
B'Tselem, 79–80
Bush, George W./Bush administration: Afghanistan invasion and, 14, 161–62n11; Afghanistan reconstruction and, 15–16; anti-Iran rhetoric of, 44, 45, 55–56, 166n1; anti-Syrian rhetoric of, 69, 69–70; congressional elections (2006) and, 26; cost-shifting by, 22; democracy export policy of, 1–2; federal crimes committed by, 32; foreign policy style of, 7–8; impeachment of, 32; Iraq invasion and, 26–27, 29; Iraq invasion plans of, 17, 30–32, 161–62n11, 165n15; Iraq studies commissioned by, 165n15; Iraq "surge" policy of, 38–39; Israeli settlements and, 80; Israeli withdrawal from Gaza and, 77, 78–79, 80–81; Israel-Lebanon war supported by, 170–71n10; provincial arrogance of, 7; Sudan sanctions extended by, 106; transparency lacking in, 6–7; world opinion of, 7

Calderoli, Roberto, 127
Caligula (Camus), 164n27
Camp David accords (2000), 83
Camp Eggers (Kabul), 23
Camus, Albert, 14, 164n27
capitalist exploitation, 136
cartoons, political: history of, 124–25. *See also* Muhammad, cartoons depicting
Cassirer, Ernst, 114, 141
Catholic Church, 135–36, 140–42. *See also* Ratzinger, Josef
CBS, 20
censorship, 168n5
Central African Republic, 102
Central Asia, U.S. military bases in, 20
Centre for Research on Globalization, 168n20
Chalabi, Ahmad, 30, 38
chameleon effect, 115–16
Cheney, Dick: anti-Iran rhetoric of, 47, 55; Iraq invasion and, 30, 31; Israel-Lebanon war and, 170–71n10; as true believer, 9
Chernobyl, 46
China: African initiatives of, 106, 107; arms sales by, 104; as Iranian trade partner, 53; as nuclear power, 48; U.S. military action against Iran and, 54
Chomsky, Noam, 162n16
Chossudovsky, Michel, 168n20
Churchill, Winston, 109, 137
CIA, 32

INDEX

citizen diplomacy: Arab media portrayals of, 3–4; benefits of, 5; defined, 2–3; in Iran, 41–42; in Palestine, 75; right-wing criticism of, 3; in Sudan, 96–99; in Syria, 59–60, 73
civic religion, 142
civil liberties: democracy dependent on, 10; harm principle and, 150–51; prepolitical values and, 142; resistance and, 124, 154; responsibility in exercise of, 124, 131; rule of law and, 155–56; U.S. wartime suspensions of, 168n5
civil rights movement, 168n5
civil society, 9, 10, 147
civil war: in Afghanistan, 18, 163n25; in Algeria, 62; American, 168n5; in Iraq, 25, 28–29, 34–36; in Lebanon, 59, 65; in Palestine, 89; in Sudan, 97
Clarke, Richard C., 161–62n11
"clash of civilizations": Afghanistan invasion and, 162n14; cartoon controversy and, 123, 129; neoconservative belief in, 13, 55; secularism vs. religious fundamentalism as, 5, 145
Clinton, Bill, 96, 162n16
Clooney, George, 105
"coalition of the willing," 38
cold war, 168n5
Columbia University, 75
common good, the, 144–45
communism, 139–40
communitarianism, 149–50
Comprehensive Peace Agreement (2006), 94, 95
Congo, 105
Conscience International, 3, 41, 96, 99
Convention on the Prevention of Genocide (1948), 172n9
Conyers, John, 32, 166n25
Corrie, Rachel, 124
cosmopolitan sensibility, 4–5; defined, 6; in Iran, 50; need for, 6; philosophical basis for, 157–60; political cartoons and, 125; true believers vs., 8–9
Council for International People's Friendship, 96
Cuban missile crisis (1962), 61
cultural insensitivity, 9
cultural uniqueness, 148–50
Cyrus the Great, 49, 50

Damascus Declaration, 63
Danish People's Party, 127
Darfur Peace Agreement (2006), 94, 95, 107
Darfur (Sudan): administrative divisions, 93; competing interests in, 100–101; as designer crisis, 105; diplomacy needed in, 107–8; genocide in, 102, 172–73n9; IDPs in, 93–95, 96, 103, 107; Khartoum government campaigns against, 93–94, 97; Khartoum government flexibility on, 97–99, 105; military intervention called for, 105–7; proposed solutions for, 101–4; regional impact of, 102; relief efforts in, 102–3; secession of, 95; UN intervention in, 96, 106–7; U.S. foreign policy failure and, 1; war crimes in, 103, 173n11; world opinion and, 104–5

Daumier, Honoré, 124
Davidson, Lawrence, 62
Dawa, 166n3
Dearlove, Richard, 31
democracy: Catholic Church opposed to, 140–41; church/state separation in, 136, 143–44; defined, 152–53; external pressure and, 65; Islamic, 64; preconditions for, lacking in Middle East, 10–11, 19, 62–63; prepolitical values and, 147; regime change as precondition for, 20–21; religion and, 131, 142; science and, 139; socialist understanding of, 151–52; tolerance in, 153–54
democracy, export of: Bush administration support for, 1–2; Iraq invasion justified by, 33–38; neoconservative belief in, 7, 9, 10–11
Democratic Party, 8
Deng, Aldondoni, 97
Dewey, John, 151
diplomacy, U.S., 5–6, 96–97. *See also* citizen diplomacy
dissent, 152; in Iran, 50–51, 53, 157, 167n9; in Syria, 63. *See also* diversity; resistance
diversity: minority rights and, 152–53; reciprocity and expression of, 150–52; resistance involved in, 149–50; rule of law and, 154–56
DNA, 143
Dosa, Abdelrahman, 97
double standards: Israeli, 175n16; Muslim fanatic, 130–31, 156; political dangers of, 156
double standards, U.S.: national security, 61; nuclear weapons, 47–48, 56–57, 138; torture, 23–24, 61
Downing Street memo, 30–32, 166n25
Dreyfus affair, 140
drug trafficking, 19, 162–63n20
Druse, Lebanese, 66
Dworkin, Richard, 131

East Jerusalem, 83
Ebadi, Shirin, 167n9
Egypt, 26, 63, 110
Einstein, Albert, 143
Eisner, Will, 125
Elseed, Nasir, 97
empiricism, 143–44, 177n6
Enlightenment fundamentalism, 135, 145
Enlightenment legacy: fear of, U.S. foreign policy failure and, 9; political aims of, 154; radical project of, truncated, 136–37; Ratzinger's views on, 135–36, 144; religion vs., 1, 135; secularism, 141, 157
Enron scandal, 32
Erdogan, Recep Tayyip, 56
Ethiopia, 102
ethnic cleansing, 75
ethnic hatreds, 93
Europe: anti-Semitism in, 113–15, 116–17; cartoon controversy in, 68–69, 128; Muslim public opinion in, 175n6; religious roots of, 135–36
European Union, Darfur crisis and, 98, 172–73n9
exceptionalism, 148

Faculty for Israeli-Palestinian Peace, 3, 75
failed states index, 16
faith: authoritarianism and, 145; knowledge vs., 142, 143, 176n2; morality and, 143–44; as private matter, 147; reason vs., 135. *See also* religion
Falluja (Iraq): insurgency resurgence in, 36; U.S. attack on (2005), 7, 27; white phosphorus used on, 27
fanaticism, 121; word and deed equated in, 124
Fanaticism or Mahomet the Prophet (Voltaire), 124
Farrow, Mia, 105
fascism, 112, 113
Fatah, 84–85, 89, 90–91
fatwas, 142
Federation of Workers' Councils and Unions of Iraq, 34
Feith, Douglas, 170n4
Ford, Henry, 109
foreign policy: of Bush administration, 6–7; cosmopolitan sensibility in, 6; style in, 7–8
Foucault, Michel, 149
France, 104, 106, 175n6
Franklin, Benjamin, 143
Franks, Tommy, 15
freedom, 144–45, 153
free speech, responsibility and, 124, 129–30
fundamentalism, 158. *See also* Enlightenment fundamentalism; Islamic fundamentalism

Galbraith, Peter, 166n3
Galileo, 143
Gandhi, Mohandas, 125, 131
Gaza: as buffer zone, 82; cartoon protests in, 129; impact of Israeli incursions in, 79–80; instability of, 89; Israeli assault on, 77, 78, 82, 86, 110; Israeli settlements and, 169–70n3; population transfers to, 82; remilitarization of, 82
Gaza, Israeli withdrawal from: Bush administration and, 78–79, 80–81; Israeli right-wing reaction to, 79; Israel-Lebanon war and, 86–88; Israel/Palestine peace process and, 78; original Israeli conception of, 76; Palestinian infighting and, 89, 90–91; Sharon and, 77–78; two-state solution and, 82–84; ulterior motives for, 81–82; unrealistic expectations and, 83
genocide, 102, 105, 115–16, 172–73n9
genomes, 143
German Empire, collapse of, 111
Germany, 130, 175n6
Global Darfur Day (Sept. 17, 2006), 104
globalization, 18, 62, 129
Goethe, Johann Wolfgang, 48
Golan Heights, 71, 87
Gorenberg, Gershom, 171n11
Goss, Porter, 56
Goya y Lucientes, Francisco José de, 124
Graham, Bob, 15
Gramsci, Antonio, 87, 139
Great Britain, 130, 143–44, 163n26, 175n6
Greater Israel, 78, 79, 118
Great in the Small, The (Nihlus), 109

Grosz, George, 124–25
Guantanamo Bay, torture at, 7, 23
Gulf War (1991), 25

Haas, Richard, 47
habeas corpus, suspension of, 168n5
Habermas, Jürgen, 176n2
Haditha (Iraq), massacre at, 7, 28
Hafez (Iranian poet), 48, 50
Halliburton, 33
Hama (Syria), 59
Hamas: Arab sympathy for, 87; electoral victory of, 69, 76, 84–86, 128, 171–72n19; Iranian support for, 44, 52, 69; Israeli refusal to negotiate with, 86, 88–89; Palestinian infighting and, 89, 90–91; Syrian support for, 69–70; U.S. foreign policy failure and, 1
Hariri, Rafiq, assassination of, 65–69, 70
Hariri, Saad, 66, 68
harm principle, 150–51
hate crime legislation, 131–32
hate speech legislation, 126, 130
Hegel, G. W. F., 116
Heidegger, Martin, 138–39
Hersh, Seymour M., 161–62n11, 170–71n10
Herzl, Theodor, 111
Hezbollah: Arab sympathy for, 87; Iranian support for, 44, 52, 69, 167n6, 170n6; Israeli soldiers kidnapped by, 76–77, 79, 86; Israel-Lebanon war and, 86–87, 170n5, 170–71n10; military power of, 170n6; Syrian support for, 65–66, 69–70; U.S. foreign policy failure and, 1
Hiroshima, U.S. bombing of, 138
Hitler, Adolf, 113, 139, 140
Hizbullah. *See* Hezbollah
Holocaust, 115, 116, 120; denial, 111, 117, 130–31
Horkheimer, Max, 139
Horse without a Horseman (Egyptian soap opera), 110
Hugo, Victor, 164n27
human rights: cosmopolitan sensibility and, 6; double standards vs., 156; as Enlightenment legacy, 136; Iranian contempt for, 53–54; Israeli abuses of, 79–80; liberal secular state and, 148; resistance and, 154; Sudanese abuses of, 100, 102, 105, 172–73n9; universal underpinnings of, 147–48, 159–60; U.S. disregard for, 1, 22–23
Human Rights Watch, 23
Huntington, Samuel, 13. *See also* "clash of civilizations"
Hurricane Katrina (2005), 41, 54
Husbaya (Iraq), 69
Hussam, Hussam Taher, 68

idealism, philosophical, 177n6
IDPs (internally displaced persons). *See* Darfur (Sudan), IDPs in
imperialism, 43; "clash of civilizations" and, 5; democracy export and, 9; Enlightenment legacy unable to eradicate, 136; in political cartoons, 125; poverty/instability as legacy of, 137; Sudanese anti-Western sentiments and, 95, 99–100, 101; Syria as product of, 168n1
Independent, 165n21

India: cartoon protests in, 128; Islamic democracy in, 64; as nuclear power, 48; U.S. military action against Iran and, 54
Indonesia, 64, 128
"In Pursuit of Peace" (Ratzinger), 136, 137–45
Institute for Advanced Strategic and Political Studies, 170n4
Institute for Internal Peace and Dialogue, 96
intellectual laziness, 121
internally displaced persons (IDPs). *See* Darfur (Sudan), IDPs in
International, Second, 174n3
International Atomic Energy Agency (IAEA), 46, 55, 166n1
International Covenant on Civil and Political Rights, 23
International Criminal Court, 68, 103, 173n11
International Human Rights Conference (2003), 41
internationalism, 156
international law: Iraq invasion as contravention of, 29–30; regime change in, 29–30; self-defense allowed in, 14
international peace organizations, Darfur crisis and, 104
Internet, 6, 60
Intifada, Second, 81
intolerance, 136, 156
Iran: Afghani refugees in, 18; alliance with Syria, 52–53, 69–70; anti-Semitism in, 44, 45, 46, 53–54, 109–10; anti-Western foreign policy of, 45–46; arms sales by, 87; authoritarian tendencies in, 45–46, 50–51, 53–54; citizen diplomacy in, 41–42; consequences of military action against, 54; cosmopolitan sensibility in, 50; cultural heritage of, 48–50; dissent in, 50–51, 53, 157, 167n9; economy of, 46; elections in, 46, 50; geopolitical situation of, 48, 52; Hamas supported by, 52; Hezbollah supported by, 52, 167n6; influence of Western imperialism on, 43; Iraq invasion and, 52; Iraqi Shiites supported by, 34, 38, 166n3; Israel-Lebanon war and, 170n5, 170–71n10; modernity vs. tradition in, 43; nuclear policies of, 41, 43, 44–48, 56–57, 166n1, 166–67n6; preemptive strike possibilities against, 41–42, 45, 47, 167n9, 168n20; reformism and corruption in, 51–52; as regional power, 44, 70, 166n4; as rogue state, 45, 47; UN sanctions against, 48; U.S. foreign policy failure in, 1, 56–57, 166–67n6; in U.S. popular imagination, 44
Iranian Revolution (1979), 52, 53
Iran-Iraq War (1980–81), 29, 44, 59, 70
Iran National Museum, 49
Iraq: anti-Semitism in, 109; Bush administration cost-shifting in, 22; Bush administration "surge" policy in, 38–39; casualties in, 10, 27; civil war in, 25, 28–29, 34–36; conditions under Saddam, 25, 33; constitution of, 33, 36; corruption in, 27–28; de-Baathification in, 28; democratic preconditions absent in, 21; as

failed state, 16; fraudulent elections in, 33; future prospects for, 37; geopolitical situation of, 168n1; governmental legitimacy in, 35–36; Iranian influence in, 166n3; Islamic jihadists in, 32; militias in, 35–36; post-invasion economy, 33–34; prisoner torture in, 28; al Qaeda supposedly linked to, 19–20, 26, 30, 32–33; reconstruction of, 27, 38; Syria-U.S. relations and, 70; U.S. foreign policy failure in, 1, 37–39; U.S. military bases in, 45, 52. *See also* Iran-Iraq War; Iraqi insurgency

Iraq, U.S. invasion of: anti-Semitism resulting from, 110; Bush administration lies preceding, 7, 30–32; Bush victory proclamation, 26–27; casualties resulting from, 27, 165n21; consequences of, 25, 32; cost of, 28–29, 38, 54; democracy as justification for, 33–38; Democratic support for, 8; as distraction from Afghanistan, 16, 161–62n11; Downing Street memo and, 30–32, 166n25; environmental effects of, 7; Hariri assassination and, 69; illegality of, 29–30; Iranian influence and, 166n4; oil and, 9, 28, 33, 34, 37; planning for, 16, 17, 30–32, 161–62n11, 165n15; sectarian conflict resulting from, 28, 33, 34–36, 44; "shock and awe" used in, 29; Sudanese anti-Western sentiments and, 95; unintended consequences of, 44; as U.S. foreign policy mistake, 37–39; in U.S. public opinion, 41; U.S. self-criticism lacking on, 37; world opinion of, 36–37

Iraqi insurgency: civil war and, 34–36; as model for Afghanistan, 19; resurgence of, 36; rise of, 21, 25; Syrian support for, 70; U.S. efforts to quell, 28; U.S. occupation fueling, 36–37

Iraq Special Commandos Unit, 36

Iraq Study Group, 38, 70

Irving, David, 130

Islam: Afghanistan invasion and Western conflict with, 162n14; external pressures and appeal of, 45; in European public opinion, 175n6; fatwas, 142; Jewish conspiracy theories questioned, 157; Shiite, 170n6; war on terror and, 127–28. *See also* Islamic fundamentalism

Islamic Brotherhood, 59

Islamic fundamentalism: cartoon controversy and, 123, 129–31, 132; "clash of civilizations" and, 5, 13; double standards in, 130 31, 156; economic globalization and, 18; Iraq invasion and, 32; 9/11 attacks and, 13; rise of, 18, 32, 53–54; Sudanese regime change and, 95–96; Syrian "state of emergency" and, 62–63

Islamic Jihad: Iranian support for, 167n6; Israeli response to, 79; Israeli soldiers kidnapped by, 76–77, 79, 86, 88; peace negotiations subverted by, 89

Islamic law, 36, 64

Islamic Party (Egypt), 63

Islamic Socialist Party (Sudan), 97

Israel: anti-Semitism vs. criticism

of, 110–11, 117–21; collective punishment policies of, 77; diminishing status of, 77, 79; economic growth in, 84; ethnic cleansing policies of, 75; Greater Israel, 78, 79, 118; Hamas refusal to recognize, 88–89; Hamas victory and, 76, 84–86; Hezbollah military power and, 170n6; Iranian call for elimination of, 45, 53–54, 110; Iran nuclear policy condemned by, 43; Iran preemptive strike possibility, 41, 43, 45, 47, 55, 168n20; military power of, 117–18; as nuclear power, 48; "Prisoner's Manifesto" and, 90–91; public opinion in, 171n11; refusal to negotiate with Hamas, 86; refuseniks in, 157; "revisionist" history in, 174n13; soldier kidnappings, 76–77, 86–87, 88; Syrian assaults on, 59; terrorist threat to, 89; two-state solution supported in, 84; wall of separation, 76, 80, 81, 83, 85. *See also* Gaza, Israeli withdrawal from; Israeli settlements; Israel-U.S. alliance; Lebanon, Israeli invasion of (2006)

Israeli Arabs, 82, 174n13, 175n16

Israeli settlements, 83; anti-Semitism and, 118; Hamas victory and, 85; history of, 171n11; Israeli policy held hostage by, 79; Palestinian fragmentation and, 76, 80, 169–70n3; populations of, 80; removal from Gaza (2005), 76; West Bank expansions, 81, 118, 170n3

Israel-U.S. alliance: arms sales, 87–88, 169n1; economic aid, 81, 83; Iranian nuclear controversy and, 43; Iran-Syria alliance strengthened by, 69–70; Israeli settlements and, 81; Lebanon invasion and, 87–88; Palestine and, 83; Palestinian government destabilized by, 76; Sudanese anti-Western sentiments and, 95, 99; world opinion of, 1

Janjaweed, 93–94, 97, 102

Jaurés, Jean, 151

Jayousz (Palestine), 75, 78–79

Jenin (Palestine), 75

Jennings, James, 41, 96

Jericho (Palestine), 78–79, 80

Jerusalem, 85

Jewish Institute for National Security Affairs (JINSA), 55

John Paul II, Pope, 141

Johns Hopkins University, 27

Johnson, Chalmers, 21, 163n25

Jones, Ann, 162n18

Jordan, 27, 56, 132

Jünger, Ernst, 113

Justice and Equality Movement, 95

Jyllands-Poste (Danish tabloid), 125–27

Kabul (Afghanistan), 23, 163n25

Kagan, Robert, 106

Kalandia (Palestine), 83

Kant, Immanuel, 6, 155

Karzai, Hamid, 19

Katrina. *See* Hurricane Katrina (2005)

Kennedy, John F., 61

Kenya, 102, 128

Khaddam, Abedel-Halim, 66
Khalifa, Majzou al-, 172n7
Khalil Ibrahim, 95
Khatami, Mohammed, 51–52
Khomeini, Ayatollah, 52, 53, 54
Khrushchev, Nikita, 61
Kirkuk (Iraq), 36
Kurdistan Workers' Party, 56
Kurds, 33, 34–36, 44, 60
Kuwait, 168n1

labor movement, 11, 112, 174n3
Labour Party (Great Britain), 31
Lake, Anthony, 106
law. *See* international law; rule of law
Lebanon: cedar revolution in, 65; civil war in, 59, 65; geopolitical situation of, 168n1; Hariri assassination and, 65–69; Israeli invasion of (1982), 120; Syrian withdrawal from, 65–66; Syria-U.S. relations and, 70; U.S. support of Israeli policy in, 1
Lebanon, Israeli invasion of (2006), 13; Afghanistan media coverage and, 20; anti-Semitism resulting from, 110; Bush administration support for, 169n1, 170–71n10; casualties in, 86–87; consequences of, 77; foreign influences in, 170n5; Hezbollah soldier kidnappings and, 86; Iran-Syria alliance strengthened by, 69–70; Israel/Palestine peace process and, 78; neoconservative support for, 170n4; Syrian peace initiatives ignored, 71–72; UN Security Council resolution to, 87–88; war aims, 87
Left, the: free speech vs. anti-bigotry sanctions, 124, 131–33; Iraq invasion and, 25; totalitarian trajectory of, 139–40. *See also* liberal hawks; liberalism/liberals
Levinas, Emmanuel, 125
Lewis, Bernard, 13
liberal hawks, 10–11; citizen diplomacy criticized by, 3; Darfur intervention called for by, 105–6, 107; provincial arrogance of, 7
liberalism/liberals: anti-Semitism and, 112; cartoon controversy and, 132–33; "clash of civilizations" and, 5; as elite ideology, 173–74n3; positivism and, 139; secular, 141–43; universal claims made by, 149–50. *See also* liberal secular state
liberal secular state: authoritarianism vs., 147–48; "clash of civilizations" and, 145; diversity in, 153; prepolitical foundations of, 176n2; reciprocity principle in, 150–52; religion and, 141–43, 145. *See also* rule of law
liberation theology, 140–41
Libi, Ibn al-Shaykh al-, 26
Libya, 129
Likud Party (Israel), 78, 79
limits, 22
Locke, John, 144, 153
Logos (journal), 75
Luxemburg, Rosa, 151

Maale Adumim, 83
majority rule, 152–53
Malawi, 105
Malley, Robert, 171–72n19

Mann, Thomas, 145
Manyang, Charles, 97
Marcuse, Herbert, 129, 155
Marshall Plan, 137
Marxism, 139, 173n3
materialism, 177n6
Matzah of Zion, The (Tlas), 109–10
McCarthyism, 168n5
media: Arab, 3–4; Israeli, 78; sensationalist, and cartoon controversy, 126–27, 129. *See also* Muhammad, cartoons depicting
media, U.S.: Afghanistan coverage of, 20; Darfur crisis and, 105; Iran preemptive strike demanded in, 41, 43; Iraq coverage of, 25, 30; Israel coverage of, 77; misinformation generated by, 4; Palestine coverage of, 76
Mehlis, Detlev, 67, 68
MEK. *See* Mujahedin-e Khalq (MEK)
Mezan Center for Human Rights in Gaza, 79–80
Middle East: anti-Semitism in, 117; arbitrary borders in, 93; modernity vs. tradition in, 43; preconditions for democratic change lacking in, 10–11; time as perceived in, 49; U.S. military bases in, 20. *See also specific conflicts and countries*
militias, 19, 35–36
Mill, John Stuart, 150–51
Miller, Judith, 30
minority rights, 152–53
Miserables, Les (Hugo), 164n27
MK77 bombs, 165n21
Mofid University (Qom, Iran), 41
Monroe Doctrine, 61
morality, faith and, 143–44
moral reason, 144
Mortazavi, Saeed, 53
Mossadegh, Mohammed, 44
Mosul (Iraq), 27
Mubarak, Hosni, 63
Muhammad, cartoons depicting: anti-Islamic intent behind, 127–28; artistic context of, 124–25; as blasphemy, 126; first Danish publishing of, 125–27; free speech vs. responsibility and, 129–30, 131–33; Hariri assassination and, 68–69; Islamic demonstrations against, 123, 127; Islamic fanatic manipulation of, 123, 129–31; media sensationalism and, 126–27, 129; pedagogical purpose and, 126; reprints of, 126–27
Muhammad, Ratzinger's comments on, 136
Mujahedin-e Khalq (MEK), 167n9
mujahideen, 163–64n26
Mullah Omar, 14
Musharraf, Pervez, 128
Muslim Brotherhood, 63
Mussolini, Benito, 140
Mustafa, El-Tijani, 97

nachbar, 174n13
Nagasaki, U.S. bombing of, 138
napalm bombs, 165n21
Natanz (Iran), nuclear reactor construction at, 41, 43, 54
National Congress Party (Sudan), 97
nationalism: anti-Semitism and, 113; "clash of civilizations" and, 5; in Iran, 43, 46–47, 52–54;

in Israel, 79; meaninglessness of, in Afghanistan, 18; "Protocols" and, 113; rise of, and U.S. foreign policy failure, 1; in U.S., foreign interventions and, 55
national self-determination, 46, 100
NATO, 17, 106
Nazism, 112, 113, 114, 125
NBC, 20
neoconservatism/neoconservatives: anti-Syrian rhetoric of, 72; citizen diplomacy criticized by, 3; "clash of civilizations" theory of, 13, 55; Darfur intervention called for by, 106, 107; democracy export and, 7, 10–11; Iran preemptive strike and, 41–42, 55–56; Iraq invasion and, 25, 30; Israeli aggressions supported by, 170n4; Israeli withdrawal from Gaza and, 78–79; "Mission Accomplished" speech and, 26; provincial arrogance of, 7; as true believers, 9; U.S. foreign policy control ended, 38. *See also* Bush, George W./Bush administration
neo-Nazis, 130
Netanyahu, Benjamin, 55, 82
New York Times, 30, 77, 98, 166n4, 169–70n3
Nigeria, 129
nihilism, 154
Nihlus, Sergi, 109
9/11 attacks. *See* September 11, 2001, attacks
Nishida Kitarō, 157
nuclear weapons: Iranian construction of, 41, 43, 44–48, 56–57, 166n1, 166–67n6; as symbolic currency, 47–48; Syrian nuclear-free initiative, 71; U.S. double standards on, 47–48, 56–57, 138
Nur, Abdelwahid Mohamed al-, 95

Occupied Territories. *See* Gaza; Gaza, Israeli withdrawal from; Palestine; West Bank
oil: Afghanistan invasion and, 15; in Ahmadinejad's electoral campaign, 52; boycotts, 53, 106; Iraq invasion and, 9, 28, 33, 34, 37; prices, Iranian manipulation of, 54; in Sudanese southern provinces, 93, 95; Syrian annexation of Lebanon and, 66; war on terror and, 7
Olmert, Ehud, 85–86, 170n3
Oman, 56
open society, 156
opium trafficking, 19, 162–63n20
Opus Dei, 114
"other, the": civil liberties and, 124; human rights and, 154; legal recognition of, 131–32, 151; liberal secular state and, 152; in political cartoons, 125; reciprocity principle and, 150–52, 159; universals and repression of, 149
Ottoman Empire, collapse of, 111, 168n1, 174n5
"outsiders." *See* "other, the"

Pakistan: Afghani mujahideen supported by, 163n26; Afghani refugees in, 18; cartoon riots in, 128–29; as nuclear power, 48; U.S. military action against Iran and, 54

Palestine: citizen diplomacy in, 75; civil war possibility in, 89; economy of, 83; fragmentation and sovereignty of, 81, 83, 169–70n3; Hamas victory in, 84–86, 128, 171–72n19; Israeli occupation costs, 84; in Israeli public opinion, 171n11; political infighting in, 70, 89; "Prisoner's Manifesto" and, 90–91; resistance groups in, 81–82; right of return, 80, 83, 85; two-state solution, 82–84; U.S. support of Israeli policy in, 1; wall of separation, 76, 80, 81, 83, 85. *See also* Gaza, Israeli withdrawal from
Palestinian Authority, 81–82, 170n4, 171–72n19
Palestinian refugees, 75, 83, 118
Palmer raids, 168n5
Pashtun (Afghani tribe), 18
Pathans, 162n17
Perle, Richard, 47, 170n4
Persepolis, 49–50
pesh merga (Kurdish militia), 36
Pew polls, 109, 175n6
phosphorus, white, 27
Pipes, Daniel, 127
Plame, Valerie, 32
plebiscites, 152
Plot, The (Eisner), 125
Poland, 117
politics, symbolic vs. practical, 123
Pol Pot, 140
Popper, Karl, 156
positivism, 139, 143–44, 177n6
postmodernism, 144
poststructuralism, 149–50
Powell, Colin, 30, 33, 70–71
power, exercise of: al-Assad (Hafez) and, 59; civil liberties as resistance to, 124; Enlightenment ethos vs., 136; limits to, 6, 22, 164n27; reciprocity principle vs., 153–54; rule of law vs., 147; torture as, 22
pragmatism, 143–44, 149–50
prejudice, 156
prepolitical values, 136, 142–43, 147, 176n2
prisoner rendition, 22–23, 26, 68–69
"Prisoner's Manifesto," 90–91
Project for the New American Century, 30
proletariat, 111–12, 173n3
proportionality, 15, 22, 161n2
"Protocols of the Elders of Zion, The": cartoons criticizing, 125; chameleon effect in, 115–16; current relevance of, 120–21; European popularity of, 109, 114–16; as explanatory device, 111–13; genocide and, 115; Middle Eastern popularity of, 109–10; as myth, 113, 114–15, 119; pedagogical purpose and, 126; political purposes of, 111. *See also* anti-Semitism
provincialism: authoritarianism and, 4; Bush administration Iraq strategy and, 7; Enlightenment legacy unable to eradicate, 136; rise of, and U.S. foreign policy failure, 1; of U.S. diplomats, 96–97; "us vs. them" mentality and, 3
public opinion, Arab, 10
public opinion, U.S.: Abu Ghraib torture scandal in, 61; Bush administration manipulation of,

32–33; congressional elections (2006) and, 26; Iran in, 44; Iraq–al Qaeda link in, 19–20; Iraq invasion in, 26; war culture in, 24
Pushtuns, 162n17

al Qaeda: 9/11 attacks and, 13, 161n2; as blowback example, 164n26; creation of, 162n16; impact of Afghanistan invasion on, 14; Iraq invasion as distraction from, 16; supposed links to Iraq, 19–20, 26, 30, 32–33; Taliban protection of, 13–14; as transnational organization, 14
Qom (Iran), 41, 147
Qualquilya (Palestine), 78–79

Rabin, Yitzhak, 79
racism, 23, 113, 131
Ramadi (Iraq), 7
Ramallah (Palestine), 67
Rathenau, Walther, 114–15
rationalism, 149–50
Ratzinger, Josef: as conservative, 135; elected pope, 135; Enlightenment legacy as viewed by, 135–36, 144; Islam as viewed by, 136; philosophical influences on, 138–39; on reason/religion balance, 138–40, 176n2
Rawls, John, 149
Reagan (Ronald) administration, 163–64n26
reason: democracy and, 143–44; faith vs., 135, 176n2
reasonable culpability, principle of, 14–15, 86
reciprocity, 150–52, 153–54, 156, 157
regime change: in Afghanistan, 16, 20–21; consequences of U.S. belief in, 1–2, 7; democracy not resulting from, 21; foreign policy alternatives to, 48; in Iran, 43, 51, 55; in Iraq, 16, 31; justifications for, in international law, 29–30, 31; in Sudan, 95–96, 107–8; in Syria, 70
relief agencies, Darfur crisis and, 100, 102–3
religion: cartoon controversy and, 132–33; civic, 142; "clash of civilizations" and, 145; democracy and, 131, 142; Enlightenment legacy vs., 1, 135, 157; fundamentalist, 158; knowledge vs., 143, 176n2; liberal secular state and, 141–43, 147; reciprocity principle and, 157; symbolic politics and, 123. *See also* faith; *specific religions*
religious intolerance, 136
"Report for the New American Century of 2000," 30
"repressive tolerance," 129, 155
resistance, 149–50, 154, 155. *See also* dissent
Rice, Condoleezza, 47, 73, 80, 171n10
Rice, Susan, 106
Richards, David, 17
Right, the: anti-Semitism and, 112; cartoon controversy and, 123, 127, 128, 130; Catholic Church and, 140–41; citizen diplomacy as viewed by, 3; Israeli settlements and, 78, 118; proportionality rejected by, 22; totalitarian trajectory of, 140. *See also* neoconservatism/neoconservatives

Rizgat tribe, 107
Robbins, Bruce, 75
rogue states, 3, 45, 47, 48, 72
Roosevelt, Franklin D., 137
Rose, Flemming, 127
Rosenberg, Alfred, 113
Royal Air Force, 31
Rubenstein, Alvin Z., 162n17
rule of law: civil liberties and, 155–56; diversity and, 153; false antinomy in, 154–55; as foundation of freedom, 144; harm principle and, 150–51; as precondition for diversity, 154–55; proportionality/limits in, 22; Ratzinger's views on, in non-Western world, 137–38; religion and, 137–38, 142; tradition vs., 153; universal underpinnings of, 147–48, 150–52
Rumsfeld, Donald, 26, 30, 33
Russia: anti-Semitism in, 117; arms sales by, 53, 104; as nuclear power, 48; U.S. military action against Iran and, 54. *See also* Soviet Union
Russian Empire, collapse of, 111
Russian Revolution (1905), 111
Russian Revolution (1917), 113, 139
Russo-Japanese War, 111
Rycroft, Matthew, 31

Saad-Ghorayeb, Amal, 170n5
Saddam Hussein: living conditions under, 25, 33; al Qaeda supposedly linked to, 30; U.S. support of, 29, 44; WMDs supposedly held by, 29, 165n15
Sadr, Moqtada al-, 166n3
Said, Edward, 120, 152
Samarra (Iraq), 27
Saudi Arabia, 56
Savyed Renaissance, 50
Second Treatise (Locke), 153
secularism: authoritarian traditionalism vs., 156–57; Catholic criticism of, 141; "clash of civilizations" and, 5, 145; as "deracinated hubris," 152; as Enlightenment legacy, 157; spirituality vs., 135. *See also* liberal secular state
Senate Select Committee on Intelligence, 30
September 11, 2001, attacks: anti-Semitism following, 109–10; Bush administration exploitation of, 17; reasons for, 13; religion and, 138; responsibility for, in U.S. popular imagination, 19–20; U.S. reaction following, 13–14
Shaath, Nabil, 26
Shah Pahlavi, 44
Shalit, Gilad, 86, 88
sharia (Islamic law), 36, 64
Sharon, Ariel, 77–78, 80–81
Sheeba Farms (Lebanon), 88
Shiite Islam, 170n7
Shiite-Sunni sectarian conflict, 28, 33, 34–36, 44
Shufat refugee camp (Palestine), 83
Silverberg, Kristen, 173n13
Sistani, Ayatollah Ali, 129
Smith, Michael, 31
socialism, 112, 151–52
social justice, 10
Sorel, Georges, 113

South Africa News, 98
South Africa Press, 172–73n9
Soviet Union: Afghanistan war/occupation and, 17–18, 21, 163–64nn25–26; mujahideen terrorist activities within, 163–64n26; Syrian cold war alliance with, 59. *See also* Russia
Spain, 175n6
Spanish Civil War, 140
Spanish Falange, 114
Sperber, Manes, 91
Spiegelman, Art, 125
spirituality, secularism vs., 135
Sri Lanka, 128
Steele, Jonathan, 172–73n9
stem cell research, 143
Stinnes, Hugo, 114
Strait of Hormuz, Iranian shutdown of, 54
Streicher, Julius, 125
Sturmer, Der (Nazi tabloid), 125
Sudan: anti-Western sentiments in, 95, 99–100, 101; arms sales to, 103–4; cartoon protests in, 128–29; citizen diplomacy in, 96–99; civil war in, 97; economic sanctions on, 106; Islamic-Arab/African intersection in, 93; national sovereignty concerns in, 101; pharmaceutical factory bombing in (1998), 96, 162n16; regime change in, 95–96, 107–8; repression in, 95; U.S. foreign policy failure in, 1, 173n13; war crimes in, 103. *See also* Darfur
Sudanese Liberation Movement, 95
Sudanese refugees, 102
suicide bombings, 89
Sunday Times, 31
Sunnis. *See* Shiite-Sunni sectarian conflict
Supreme Council for the Islamic Revolution, 44, 166n3
Sweden, anti-Semitism in, 175n16
Syria: alliance with Iran, 52–53, 69–70; alliance with Soviet Union, 59; arms sales by, 87; authoritarian legacy of, 59; citizen diplomacy in, 59–60, 73; democratic reforms in, 60–64, 65; dissent in, 63; forty-year "state of emergency" in, 60, 61–63; geopolitical situation of, 72, 168n1; Hariri assassination and, 65–69; Iraq invasion and, 52; Iraqi Sunnis supported by, 38; Israel-Lebanon war and, 170nn4–5, 170–71n10; as rogue state, 72; tribalism in, 64–65; U.S. foreign policy failure in, 1, 69–73; withdrawal from Lebanon, 65–66

Taliban: 9/11 attacks and, 161n2; appeal of, 18; as blowback example, 21, 163n25; culpability of, 15; negotiations attempted by, 14; al Qaeda protected by, 13–14, 162n16; resurgence of, 1, 16–17, 18, 21–22; U.S. negotiations with, necessary, 21–22
tax collection, 19
Taylor, Charles, 149
Tehran University, 53
terrorism: Iranian nuclear controversy and, 44, 54; Iraq invasion and increase of, 32, 36; Israeli Gaza withdrawal and, 78;

torture and, 23–24; U.S. foreign policy failure and, 1. *See also* September 11, 2001, attacks; war on terror
theocracy, Islamic, 147
Times of London, 30
Tinay, Hasim El-, 96
Tlas, Mustafa, 109–10
Tocqueville, Alexis de, 83
tolerance, 129, 153–54, 155
torture: of Afghani prisoners, 22–23; as denial of proportionality/limits, 22; in Iraq, 28; provincialism and, 7; scandals involving, 68–69; U.S. double standards on, 23–24, 61
traditionalism, 153, 154, 155, 156–57. *See also* authoritarianism
transparency, 6–7
Transparency International, 27–28
tribalism, 93, 119, 162n17
Trotsky, Leon, 19
true believers, cosmopolitan sensibility vs., 8–9
Tueni, Gebran, 68
Tulkarm (Palestine), 79
Turkey, 45, 56, 64

Uganda, 102, 105
UNESCO, 100
United Iraq Alliance, 166n3
United Nations: anti-Syrian policy in, 60; Darfur crisis and, 98–99, 106–7, 172n7, 172–73n9; Hariri assassination investigated by, 66–67; Human Misery Index, 106; human rights statements of, 148; as imperialist tool, 95, 99–100, 101; Resolution 1706, 173n13; Sudanese arms embargo, 103; weapons inspections by, 31. *See also* United Nations Security Council; *specific branches of United Nations*
United Nations Charter, 100, 161n2
United Nations General Assembly, 99–100
United Nations High Commission for Refugees, 107
United Nations Human Rights Council, 53
United Nations Security Council, 55; Darfur crisis and, 94, 173n11; Iran sanction possibility, 48; Iraq invasion unsanctioned by, 30; Israel-Lebanon war motion of, 87–88; undemocratic constitution of, 99
United States: arms sales by, 104, 138; Christian Right in, 118; church/state separation in, 143–44; consensus and political debate in, 130; Darfur crisis and, 99, 173n9, 173n13; diminishing status of, 72; diplomatic efforts of, 5–6, 96–97; domestic protest rare in, 5–6; economic sanctions imposed by, 106; exceptionalism of, 148; failed Middle East policies of, 1–2, 10–11, 37–39, 166n4, 166–67n6 (*see also specific conflicts and countries*); hate crime legislation in, 131–32; ideological conflict within, 156–57; Iran nuclear policy condemned by, 43; Iran preemptive strike possibility, 41, 45, 47, 167n9; Iraqi government dependent on, 35–36; Israel-Lebanon war and, 87, 169n1, 170–71n10;

war crimes committed by, 23; wartime civil liberties suspensions of, 168n5. *See also* Bush, George W./Bush administration; Israel-U.S. alliance
United States Air Force, 31
United States Central Intelligence Agency, 163–64nn25–26
United States Congress, Iraq nonbinding resolution of, 39
United States military: Middle Eastern bases, 20, 45, 52; NATO troops supplied by, 17; overextension of, 54; prisoner rendition, 22–23
universalism: double standards vs., 156; particular vs., 148–50; political vs. cultural arguments, 148–50; reciprocity principle, 150–52, 153–54, 156; state acceptance of, 147–48
U.S. Academics against War, 25
U.S. Academics for Peace, 41, 45–46, 59–60, 73
"us vs. them" mentality, 3

values, prepolitical, 136, 142–43, 147, 176n2
Vienna Declaration of Human Rights, 148, 149
Vietnam War, 5–6, 163n25, 168n5
Volkskunde, 113–14
Voltaire, 124, 125

Wagner, Richard, 115
war, culture of, 24
war crimes, 23, 103, 173n11
War Crimes Act, 23
War of 1812, 168n5
war on terror: Bush administration misinformation regarding, 7; Democratic support for, 8; in European Muslim public opinion, 175n6; international support needed in, 6; Iraq invasion and, 29; Islam as enemy in, 127–28
War Powers Resolution, 32
Washington Post, 166n1
Wasila, Al-Samani Al-, 98
weapons of mass destruction (WMDs), 29, 31
Weber, Max, 104, 112, 141
Weimar Republic, 140
West Bank, 80; Israeli settlements in, 118, 169–70n3; Israeli withdrawals from, 76, 85
West-Oestliche Divan (Goethe), 48
Wiesel, Elie, 105
Wilkerson, Lawrence, 33
Wolfowitz, Paul, 28, 30
world community: Darfur crisis and, 104–5; Israeli reputation sinking in, 77, 79; U.S. contempt for, 1; U.S. reputation sinking in, 4, 20, 30, 36–37
World Health Organization, 100
World War I, 111–13, 168n5
World War II, 137, 140, 168n5

xenophobia, 5, 54, 79

Yemen, 132
"Young Turks," 174n5

Zagawa tribe, 107
Zionism/Zionists, 55, 79, 111, 118, 128
Zionist Congress, First (1898), 109
Zoroaster/Zoroastrianism, 48, 50
Zundel, Ernst, 130